Management Teams

By the same author and Eunice Belbin MA PhD

PROBLEMS IN ADULT RETRAINING

Management Teams

Why They Succeed or Fail

R. MEREDITH BELBIN MA PhD

With a Foreword by Antony Jay

Butterworth-Heinemann Ltd
Linacre House, Jordan Hill, Oxford OX2 8DP

 PART OF REED INTERNATIONAL BOOKS

OXFORD   LONDON   BOSTON
MUNICH   NEW DELHI   SINGAPORE   SYDNEY
TOKYO   TORONTO   WELLINGTON

First published 1981
Reprinted 1983, 1984, 1985, 1986, 1987, 1988, 1989, 1990, 1991,
1992, 1993

ISBN 0 7506 0253 8

Printed and bound in Great Britain by
Biddles Ltd, Guildford and King's Lynn

Contents

Foreword

How many management research findings can you remember which fulfilled the following conditions?

1. A concept which is completely original.
2. Development and testing which are intellectually rigorous and academically respectable.
3. Results that are validated by successful prediction.
4. Applications that go to the very heart of management.

In my own experience, such a combination hardly occurs once in ten years. That is what gives so much fascination to Dr Meredith Belbin's research into the nature, structure and behaviour of teams, and the contrasting but complementary roles of the individuals who compose them.

But Dr Belbin's work is more than fascinating; it is also extremely timely. For too many years the search for successful management has been seen almost exclusively as a search for the right individual. Corporations have been preoccupied with the qualifications, experience, and achievement of individuals; they have applied themselves to the selection, development, training, motivation, and promotion of individuals; they have discussed and debated the strengths and weaknesses of individuals; and yet all of us know in our hearts that the ideal individual for a given job cannot be found. He cannot be found because he cannot exist.

Any attempt to list the qualities of a good manager demonstrates why he cannot exist: far too many of them are mutually exclusive. He must be highly intelligent and he must not be too clever. He must be forceful and he must be sensitive to people's feelings. He must be dynamic and he must be patient. He must be a fluent communicator and a good listener.

He must be decisive and he must be reflective; and so on. And if you do find this jewel among managers, this paragon of mutually incompatible characteristics, what will you do when he steps under a bus, or goes to live abroad for the sake of his wife's health, or leaves to take up a better job from your principal competitor?

But if no individual can combine all these qualities, a team of individuals certainly can – and often does; moreover, the whole team is unlikely to step under a bus simultaneously. This is why it is not the individual but the team that is the instrument of sustained and enduring success in management. A team can renew and regenerate itself by new recruitment as individual team members leave or retire, and it can find within itself all those conflicting characteristics that cannot be united in any single individual. It can build up a store of shared and collectively owned experience, information and judgement, and this store can be passed on as seniors depart and juniors arrive. And it can be in ten places at once.

Many of us must have perceived something of the truth about teams from our own experience. We know how often someone who has been highly successful within a team becomes a great disappointment when moved out of it. We have seen effective teams destroyed by the promotion of individuals, while nobody ever considered the alternative possibility of promoting the whole team, or enlarging its scope and responsibility. And we have also seen teams produce a quality and quantity of work far higher than the sum of what the separate individuals could have produced on their own.

This is a truth known to all of us who have ever worked in successful teams. The corollary is that, while not ignoring or neglecting the individual, we should devote far more thought to teams: to the selection, development, and training of teams, to the qualifications, experience, and achievements of teams, and above all to the psychology, motivation, composition, and behaviour of teams. But how? The trouble is that by comparison with our knowledge of individual psychology, individual motivation, and individual behaviour, our knowledge of what makes a successful team is tiny. It is because Dr Belbin has not only asked this question but come up with such a fascinating, convincing, and extensively documented answer that I believe his work to be the most important single contribution of the past decade to our understanding of how human organizations work, and how to make them work better. His researches have brought forth a rare addition to that tiny number of management classics – books that every working manager should be forced to read, if necessary at pistol-point.

ANTONY JAY

Preface

Not so long ago nearly every firm was run by a boss or a "governor" as he was sometimes quite accurately called. In every sense he was the manager. Nowadays most middle-sized and large firms, and almost all institutions, are run by small management teams. Each team member may carry the designation "manager" but the word has largely lost its original meaning: it no longer implies an authority figure and may refer merely to someone holding a position of responsibility.

The shift in power and authority away from the individual and towards a team owes something to the climate of our times. The concentration of power tends to corrupt, so that it is better to share power. The more educated the population entering into employment, the greater the desire for some say in management. On both moral and intellectual grounds it is unacceptable to many that one person should make all the important decisions. And then there is the sheer difficulty of doing so. The decision-making business has to embrace changing technology, competition that is international as well as domestic, and the administrative problems of running a company in a world that is becoming increasingly complicated. The lone helmsman, whatever his ability, is prone to mistakes and oversights which reflect the limitations of his knowledge and experience. The management team has become the stable alternative, a means of running a company effectively so long as the right combination of people can be found.

For many years the qualities of the individual manager have been a focal point of interest: those of a successful management team are less well understood. A team is more difficult to study than a person. This book takes up the challenge in an endeavour to study what makes a team "tick" and why one team achieves so much more than another.

The material which forms the body of this book is the product of over nine years of original research, most of which was conducted at the Administrative Staff College, Henley, by the Industrial Training Research Unit* from Cambridge. The work centred mainly round the composition of teams, according to various hypotheses and designs. One hundred and twenty management teams were formed in an experimental way, mostly with six members in each team. Team effectiveness was measured in terms of financial results in a management game. Another seventy "companies" composed either by the Directing Staff of the College or by the members themselves were also observed. During the later stages of the project seminars on management team-building were organized at Henley, in Cambridge, and in the leading cities of Australia, with a view to introducing to industry some of the main concepts which had developed from the work. For this purpose new exercises were introduced which enabled us to study managers working in groups of four under conditions of pressure and where co-ordination was important but difficult. We composed forty-five such teams in the UK and a further forty-seven in Australia.

Central to the approach developed as an outcome of these experiments has been the concept of team-role. This defines the ways in which members with characteristic personalities and abilities contribute to a team. Useful team-roles are limited in number and the success of a team depends on their interlocking pattern and how well they are discharged. Given certain information on the team-roles to which members of a team are predisposed by nature and ability, we can give a fair estimate of whether that team is likely to succeed or fail in meeting its objectives. Lastly, and perhaps most importantly, our team-building theories and ideas have been made operational in a number of organizations and companies in the UK and Australia.

Although this book is founded on research, it is addressed not so much to the academic world as to practising managers. In catering for their needs I have tried to steer a course between keeping close to the facts on the one hand and avoiding unnecessary detail on the other. I have also tried wherever possible to cite industrial examples from beyond the realm of team experiments and training courses. These cases are all based on personal knowledge. Where these might cause embarrassment to an individual or a firm I have thought fit to use pseudonyms.

---

* The ITRU was formerly part of University College, London and is now an independent limited company dealing with research and development.

The managers covered in this study involved both non-Caucasians and women, both in relatively small numbers. The conclusions reached, I believe, apply without regard to race or sex. On a semantic note the word *he*, where used in a general sense, refers to *man* in its broader meaning in line with the saying "man embraces woman".

Inevitably the work that is described has entailed using a number of technical terms; otherwise the reader would have faced much repetitive circumlocution. A "minor language" has therefore been used for the purpose of embodying the main ideas and concepts and for describing recurring team phenomena. Here it is hoped that the Glossary will resolve any difficulties. The intention, even if imperfectly fulfilled, has been to keep to a simple theme. With this in view and to avoid overloading the reader, I have omitted surveying the writings of others or making specific references within the text. Some readers, however, may feel stimulated to explore the subject further and to enable them to do so suggestions on additional reading are given on pp. 171-2.

The people I would like to thank in this Preface represent every aspect of the project. To start, there were those who made it possible. The Director of the ITRU, Dr Eunice Belbin (and in her private capacity my wife) managed to keep the funds going – I know not how – so that the work could continue over a long period. Eunice is also responsible for eliminating what would have been the worst pages of this book and helping me to improve others. We are both grateful to the Manpower Services Commission and its predecessors for continuous financial aid and encouragement. At the Administrative Staff College we had the good fortune to be launched by the Principal, J. P. Martin-Bates, who gave much needed support at critical stages. Later, his successor, Professor Tom Kempner, gave discerning practical advice and was one of the first to encourage us to move into a wider arena.

The first person to entice us into industry was Ian McDavid (now retired) of the British Oxygen Company. We were unprepared at the time but Ian enabled us to see the potential value to industry of what was emerging from the work. In the Southern Hemisphere I owe much to the initiative of Dr Ted Kelsall, Principal of the Australian Administrative Staff College, for setting in motion my Australian tours, to my Australian colleague, Neil Stucley, for his part in arranging and running our seminars, and to other staff at the college for their support.

As this book is about teams, it will not surprise the reader to learn that teamwork accounts for a large part of any progress we succeeded in making. The man who personally brought me to Henley in the first instance was Ben Aston, who also ran the management game and found ingenious ways of modifying the exercise to bring out points of value for management education. Another close colleague at the College was Andrew Life who is perhaps best known to members (as the course-taking managers at the College are called) as a wise counsellor and someone whose personal advice on management style is closely heeded. Andrew trained the observers in our experiments and also became an expert in interpreting material from the tests which we introduced.

In the ITRU I have been helped from start to finish (and organized in so far as this was at all possible) by Dr Jeanne Fisher, formerly an anthropologist. Jeanne has the unusual accomplishment of being equally conversant with the behaviour of primitive Kikuyu women and senior industrial executives. She developed the system of observation that we used throughout the experiments. On the statistical side we were helped for the first few years by a lady who will be remembered by many for her charming saris, Dr Saradha Supramaniam. Saradha made the first breakthrough by identifying the "Company Worker" personality characteristic of members who tended to be found in the more successful companies in the game. Later, we were fortunate in enrolling as her successor Bill Hartston. Bill, twice British Chess Champion, not only advised as to what conclusions we could legitimately reach as a result of our experiments but also showed an aptitude, unusual in a mathematician, for developing new psychometric test material. The colleague with whom I was most closely associated during the development and application of the management team concepts was Roger Mottram, Assistant Director of the ITRU and now Person-nel Director of Woolworths Ltd. (Australia). Roger came to ITRU with an already profound knowledge of psychometric tests and gave us a good basis for developing new assessment material. Together we formulated the notions that enabled us to make predictions about management team outcomes. We were, I think, virtually interchangeable as forecasters.

It is, of course, more fun making forecasts than being the object of them. The executives on the management courses at Henley played no mean part in the proceedings. We owe them a deep debt of gratitude for their forbearance in letting us observe them and "interfere" with their management education in the long term interests of greater knowledge.

My final thanks go to Antony Jay for writing the Foreword, the more so as he is himself the author of two books that are landmarks in this area, as well as being the creator of the BBC's award winning television series *Yes Minister*. Tony and I have spent hours of fruitful discussion on management teams and still find many avenues unexplored.

R. M. BELBIN

Cambridge

1: A Study of Teams: How It All Began

One day an unknown visitor came to our offices in Cambridge to discuss computer applications in management. There must have been many better places to pursue the matter, for we knew little about the subject. It was not even one that attracted us, although at the time it was very much *de rigueur*. Gradually it transpired that an application had been made for research funds to study the use of the computer in management, that the unofficial answer was a shake of the head but with a nod that pointed in our direction. If the project could be tied up in some way with the current research programme of the Industrial Training Research Unit the grant was more likely to be forthcoming. Why that should have been suggested is not clear; but that at any rate was how I met my future colleague, Ben Aston. Through his initiative and persuasion a research link was established between the Industrial Training Research Unit at Cambridge and the Administrative Staff College at Henley.

Henley, as it is referred to more succinctly, has the distinction of being the oldest management College in Europe, and is situated at the point where the Chiltern Hills tumble down towards the Thames. The College is the former home of Lord Hambleden and is a mile or so from the village that bears his name – a village that looks like a stage set for a period play but which is perhaps better known to Henley members for the relaxing atmosphere of its village pub.

To drive up to this stately home over the cattle grid, by the gatehouse, past the meadows dotted with low-branching trees, towards the fine

1

close-cropped lawns that amble down to the banks of the Thames, where swans, ducks, and wild geese noisily stake out their territories in the river against the backdrop of deserted pastures beyond; all that is to heighten man's ingenuity for finding a reason for staying a little longer than was originally intended.

But it transpired that there were more basic reasons for prolonging what might otherwise have been a fleeting visit. Henley's approach to the education of managers was founded on syndicate work. A syndicate comprised ten or eleven members, carefully selected to give a balance in terms of background and experience. They were bankers, engineers, accountants, scientists, civil servants and men with general production or commercial experience, nearly all practising managers. Most of them, in their late thirties, were being groomed for higher appointments or top management.

Syndicate operation created its own style of learning. Its advocates have argued that syndicate operation is virtually the only feasible way of creating a suitable learning environment for mature managers. At any rate the emphasis on syndicate work had led to a growing interest in the operation of management teams. The College had long recognized that some syndicates functioned better than others. The underlying reasons for this were elusive and were subject to much debate on the part of the Directing Staff. Managers who were individually able and impressive could be disappointing in combination, while other less impressive managers functioned well together. There seemed no easy way of forecasting which combinations of managers would produce the best teams.

THE EME

The advent of the management game or executive management exercise (EME) had intensified interest in the subject. Syndicates were broken up to allow their members to be re-formed into new groups, known as *companies*, for the purpose of competing in the game. Once again some management teams functioned better than others. But this time there was a material difference. The outcomes were measurable. At the conclusion of the exercise financial assets were counted. This meant that *companies* could be compared with one another along a single index of success and failure. Assessment of how well a management team functioned could therefore depend not so much on subjective impression as on the outcome. "That's what counts in Chicago", is what our American cousins teach us. Results are what managers are expected to produce, and it seemed therefore fitting to use a hard criterion as the means by which the effectiveness of Henley teams might be judged. The innovation which marked our joint investigation into management teams was that in addition to measuring the output we should measure also the input, here construed as the human resources that go into the construction of the team. Accordingly members of the teams were given a battery of psychometric tests. These in effect told us something about the personality and mental ability of each member and offered the possibility of forming particular types of team with a characteristic input pattern.

The relationship between the input and the output now became the focus of interest. The nature of this process needed to be studied and here we were assisted by observers drawn from the course members who were more interested in watching what went on in a management team than in participating as games players. The observers were trained to use a standardized method of observation whereby every half minute an entry would be made on their recording sheets of the type of contribution that a member was making. There were seven observed categories of behaviour: asking, informing, proposing, opposing, delegating, building, and commenting. The numerical scores in these categories made it possible to establish not only who was doing most of the talking but also what was the nature of the particular interventions that characterized each member. The cross-relating of the input and process data could show, for example, whether the person doing most of the proposing was one of the cleverer members, as measured by the tests, or one of the more ebullient, as measured by the personality inventory.

During the early stages of our investigations we laid ourselves open to the charge that there was something artificial about the management teams which we were studying. Our tentative conclusions were contested by some industrialists, drawn from more austere environments, who saw the stately home of the College amid its tranquil surroundings as being far removed from the reality they knew. The very location of our studies prejudiced acceptance of the phenomena we reported. Our experiments were seen by some people as being conducted under glasshouse conditions and therefore not applicable.

Before considering this objection further, it is as well to consider the nature of the demands which the management game imposed on its members. There were usually six members in a *company* and there were roles for a Chairman, a Secretary, and executives responsible for Marketing, Production, Finance, and Management Services. On most courses there were eight *companies* competing in an exercise which attempted to simulate the problems that companies experience in a world of fluctuating markets. The EME spanned a period of "three years" and the data from the "quarterly" returns were fed into a computer. The game was interactive, so that the merits of *company* decisions depended on the decisions and actions which other *companies* took in both the domestic and the export markets. *Companies* could buy market research at a price and operational research advice was also available. Finance houses and trade unions also came into the exercise as bodies with which dealings could be made. In short, members of each *company* had a certain amount of individual work to perform but at the same time their plans had to be co-ordinated if there was to be any strategic coherence in their collective decisions. What then had the EME in common with the typical problems that confront management teams in practice? It was that departmental interests and decisions had to be balanced and set against the priorities of the business as a whole. Hard data had to be considered along with uncertainty. In effect the EME was all about six people sitting round a table thrashing out problems and trying to make good decisions.

As might be expected the EME, being a computer-based game, placed an emphasis on analysis and calculation, and a modelling approach to business generally, although a range of other skills was also needed. In due course after several years of experiments with the EME we began to run seminars on management teams. For this purpose we felt a new exercise was needed in which negotiating skills would figure more strongly. Another felt need was to bring out more sharply the lessons of success and failure. Under the EME we had learned that some unsuccessful *companies* had avoided examining the underlying reasons for their poor results by seizing on gratifying excuses. The favourites were "If the game had gone on longer, we would have won," and "We would have done all right if it hadn't been for some doubtful umpiring on a critical point."

TEAMOPOLY

Part of the trouble was that differences in the final assets of *companies* were sometimes small and this created the impression that levels of effectiveness were much the same. As a means of sharpening the lessons associated with success or failure we created a new seminar exercise called Teamopoly. This was based on both the materials and mechanics of Monopoly, the well-known property game. The delightful – or chilling – point about Monopoly is that fortunes eventually become compounded, reminiscent of the Victorian song, "It's the same the whole world over ain't it all a bloomin' shame . . . It's the rich that gets the gravy and the poor that get the blame." The blame in this case fell on the *company* that finished in poverty through its own failures–very much as Victorian morality would have it.

Teamopoly differed from its parent by being a team game with four members to each *company*. The rules were revised so that property could change hands only by tender, auction, and negotiation. As a result of this and other changes, luck was to a great extent eliminated. Teamopoly presented great opportunities for human skill and ingenuity and placed teams under considerable stress. The only practical difficulty experienced was that teams could become bankrupt earlier than was desirable. This could lead to four morose managers taking up early positions at the bar. The introduction of bank loans, as a means of keeping these *companies* afloat for as long as it was psychologically desirable, eventually overcame this problem. In general the design of Teamopoly achieved its purpose in bringing home emphatically the reasons for team failures. These could usually be accounted for in faulty team composition, for which the members could not be blamed, or in a poor use of team resources, for which they could.

In Teamopoly each *company* conducted its own inquest after the game had finished. The conclusions, being public, were shared and so were able to enter into the realm of generalizable experience.

Whether basic principles exist that are transferable to the everyday workings of management teams depends in the last analysis on what happens when they are put to the test. After about five or six years of experimental work, the theories and techniques which we had pioneered at Henley were used in an increasing number of firms to develop managers, to reconstruct unsuccessful management teams, and to set up well-balanced teams for new projects and ventures. This extension of our activities has of course added to our store of knowledge. Yet with the benefit of hindsight it must be said that the great bulk of what has been learned has its roots in the original experimental work at Henley. The principles that were developed there have stood up well to the test of time and trial under very different conditions.

STAGES OF RESEARCH

The nature of the work on which we were engaged at Henley fell basically into five stages. All these stages, however, retained two common features – members, who volunteered to do so, took our battery of psychometric tests (*see* Glossary) and the financial outcomes of the various teams were measured and taken as an indication of their success in meeting their objectives.

During the first stage we accepted the teams as they had been composed by the College and were content to learn what lessons we could from the test results of the individuals comprising the teams, the observer material and the financial yardsticks at the end.

During the second stage we were allowed to compose the teams ourselves. We took advantage of the offer in the first place by assigning members with similar test scores to the same teams. This procedure allowed us, for example, to study teams of pure extroverts and pure introverts, or those high or less high in mental ability. On this last point we thought it indelicate to proceed with experiments for long! The diagram on p. 23 shows some personality trends we discovered at this stage.

During the long third stage we tested out a number of specific hypotheses. Experiments were designed accordingly. Boldly, or even recklessly, we made forecasts about the outcomes. These were transmitted to the secretary of the management game before the start of the exercise. This stage proved the most rewarding part of our work since every "error" told us something and the *company* observers gave us a lead on why things had turned out differently from our expectations. However it was already apparent that a basis was developing for the predictions.

During the fourth stage we modified our objectives to enable managers to play an active part in designing their own teams.

In the fifth and final stage we reverted for a short period to the experimental conditions of Stage Three but produced rather more sophisticated team designs which were based on what we had learned during the intervening period.

Looking back on the experiments it is plain to see that we were caught in a dilemma – trying to conduct worthwhile controlled experiments on the one hand, and on the other, setting up an experience in learning which was useful for the members. The members received the early experiments in good part at a time when we felt we knew very little. As knowledge grew we were able to put over an account of previous work together with a tentative set of general hypotheses about the characteristics of good and poor teams. Then more constraints became necessary if we were to advance our knowledge further. Some received the design features of our experiments with good humour, interest, and fascination. A few others, it must be said, expressed from time to time the feeling that they were being manipulated, acted upon by sinister forces not entirely within their control. Nearly every course contained some surprise and that offered consolation for those who preferred to hold that man was unpredictable!

The changes that allowed for more participation in team composition on the part of members (Stage Four) were initially well received. Inviting members to form their own superteam fired their imagination. The success of the members' team, which was usually composed to take account of what we had already taught them about team composition, was a form of self-vindication. *They* too could produce impressive results by creating teams of good design. But the elitist nature of this exercise produced some internal tensions in the course from which we, the experimenters, as bystanders, escaped. These tensions prompted a modification.

A new procedure was set up to allow *all* the *companies* in the management game to be picked by members nominated by each syndicate. This allowed a selector to fashion his own theories on team composition. The team selectors would meet on one fateful occasion to put into operation a team selection strategy in competition with the others. To enable them to do this the selectors had before them a set of scores based on assessments within the syndicates of the best team-role characteristics of every member on the course. The concept of a team-role is elaborated in Chapter Six.

The published summary assessments were presented by anonymous code numbers rather than by name. At selection time, the selector had no idea of the identity of the coded persons. He would examine the total list and, when his turn came, he would pick the sort of person he thought would fit in with the team he was trying to create. The outcome could be a great shock for some selectors where their concept of team design depended on personal likes or dislikes. A favourite golfing companion would be omitted whereas a member with whom a selector had clashed might be included. The advantage lay with those selectors who had thought about team design and balance in a more conceptual way.

The innovations and departures from our carefully planned experiments offered more involvement and participation and provided a good deal of enjoyment for members. That gain was made at a certain cost. Personal experience was vivid but on some courses at least, less of general transferable value was learned. Some of the members began to feel this themselves. We were pressed to return to our former and more contentious role of picking the teams according to our own design plans. "Leave it to the experts and see what they come up with," or words to that effect, began to be expressed in a regular and recurring way.

The experiments began again (Stage Five). Teams with interesting design characteristics were chosen and once more the outcomes were accounted for in terms of the differing compositions of the teams and whether or not they played to their strengths. We now knew far more about success and failure in teams. However, as we put forward our notions with greater confidence, levity fell and discomfiture increased – not on all sides but, as might be expected, in the teams that turned in poor performances. Acceptable excuses are readily found for team failures when work is at a tentative phase. Once knowledge became firmer the failure of a *company* could produce a sense of unease or even resentment. Our own role in the proceedings and outcome was exaggerated. Some felt that our ability to forecast – even though the nature of the forecast at that stage was unknown to them – could in some way restrict their power to control their own destinies.

After nine years of almost continuous work, we felt we had explored every twist and turn that we could think of in designing management teams, and we were beginning to rediscover and re-experience phenomena that we had first encountered a good deal earlier. In our final exercise at Henley, we made a very close prediction of the order of success and failure in the eight *companies* taking part. The time had come to take our leave.

Henley has a sister college in Australia, the Administrative Staff College at Melbourne, which was keen to avail itself of knowledge on the theory of the composition of effective management teams. This link resulted in three Australian tours during which the full range of team designs were tried out. Management teams "down under" behaved like their counterparts on the other side of the world. Team design stood out as a more important determinant of behaviour than hemisphere or cultural differences.

What follows in this book is an attempt to bring out the salient points about what has been learned. Experiments and industrial applications taken together at least allow some answers to the question: why do some management teams succeed and others fail?

2: The Apollo Syndrome

Given a free choice of members and the need to form a high-powered management team, how should we go about it? We know that difficult and complex problems call for sharp analytical minds. So why not create a team entirely composed of clever people, amply endowed for coping with major projects and big decisions?

The think-tank approach seems on the face of it the ideal way of harnessing human talent and using it to good effect in vital areas. A management game containing a host of complex rules, constraints, variables, and possibilities provides just such a setting in which brains are at a premium.

The welcome opportunity afforded to us by the Directing Staff at Henley to form management teams much as we liked for the EME gave us the chance to draw up teams that differed from one another in measured mental ability. Teams of clever people were formed and compared with dullard and other teams. Experimentally this was as ideal as politically it was risky. In due course a compromise was made: We were allowed to continue forming think-tank-like teams, but were prevailed upon not to form teams made up exclusively of those at the lower end of the intellectual spectrum. If mental ability was to be measured every team had to be given a fair chance of winning. Accordingly we gave an assurance that no team would be without one member whose scores were above average.

On the very first occasion when we formed a *company* of high scorers on the tests of mental ability, the members soon tumbled to what we were doing once the membership of the various *companies* chosen to compete in the exercise was made public. In the past we had designated

9

companies by letters of the alphabet–*Company* A would meet in the room normally occupied by Syndicate A, *Company* B in Syndicate B's room and so on. For a change we decided to give our *companies* names instead of the more impersonal letters. The name said something about the *company* while still indicating the room in which it should convene. For what would hitherto have been our A *company* we chose the title Apollo (chosen out of respect for the American lunar triumph at the time) and into this alpha-type *company* we placed the members who were high scoring on the measures of mental ability. The individual scores were of course confidential but there was an immediate reaction from the bulk of course members. The Apollo *company* was immediately recognized for what is was and seen as a blatant attempt by the experimenters to form a *company* that was bound to win. When very clever people are put together in a group there is no disguising the fact.

In human affairs nothing should be taken for granted. That a team of clever people should win in an exercise that placed a premium on cleverness seemed fairly obvious. Such an elementary principle was at least worth checking before any more subtle variations in team design were made. It was as well that we did. The Apollo team finished last.

There is many a slip 'twixt cup and lip in management games just as in other facets of life. The result might have been due to some chance mishap or miscalculation on some fine point. This was our immediate reaction. We changed our view when we found that the unfavourable outcome was the natural result of what from the records of the observer seemed an unsatisfactory process.

FLAWS IN APOLLO TEAMS

The Apollo team members had spent a large part of their time engaged in abortive debate, trying to persuade the other members of the team to adopt their own particular, well-stated, point of view. No one seemed to convert another or be converted. On the other hand, each seemed to have a flair for spotting the weak points of the other's argument. There was, not surprisingly, no coherence in the decisions that the team reached – or was forced to reach – and several pressing and necessary jobs were totally neglected. The eventual failure of the *company*, in finishing last in the exercise, was marked by mutual recriminations. Altogether the Apollo *company* of supposed super-talent proved an astonishing disappointment.

Promising experiments always need to be repeated. For several years we continued to construct an Apollo *company* to participate in the EME. Of twenty-five *companies* which we constructed according to our

Apollo design only three became the winning team. The favourite finishing position out of eight was sixth (six times), followed by fourth (four times). It amazed many Henley members that *companies* comprising clever people (and who were recognized as such) should collectively perform so poorly.

The occasional good result, the reason for which we will examine later, redeemed the scene. However, on average, Apollo *companies* did perform worse than other *companies* in spite of their obvious advantages.

The Apollo Syndrome also became an established phenomenon in the Teamopoly game which became a feature of the seminars we ran on management teams. If there was a chance of constructing a typical Apollo *company*, we never failed to seize it. We were seldom disappointed with the lessons that Apollo *companies* taught both their own members and the ever-interested onlookers from other *companies*. Apollo *companies* usually ran true to type – difficult to manage, prone to destructive debate and in difficulties with decision-making. Members of these *companies* acted along lines that they favoured personally without taking account of what fellow *company* members were doing. This at least circumvented the blockages caused by collective indecision, but uncoordinated action is only slightly better than taking no action at all. What one member did was undermined, usually unintentionally, by the actions of another. The lack of coherent teamwork nullified the gains of individual effort or brilliance. Apollo *companies* were frequently in cash flow problems in Teamopoly due to the competing strategic demands for whatever cash the *company* had.

Occasionally the behaviour of Apollo *companies* did not follow the typical pattern. Yet they still failed to fulfil their potential. Perhaps they had heard of and were overconscious concerning the dangers. In these instances Apollo members seemed deliberately to avoid their susceptibility to intellectual rivalry and one-upmanship. They showed undue respect for each other's proposals. Confrontation was avoided by the reluctance to admit that some proposals were mutually incompatible. This overcompensation in behaviour had a similar effect to engaging in confrontation and then ignoring the opposition, albeit a cosier one. In both instances ideas were left hanging in the air and no one understood how the various contributions had been assimilated and to what end.

SUCCESSFUL APOLLO TEAMS

Some Apollo *companies* did achieve reasonably good results and these exceptions to the rule are not without interest since they give us leads on how think-tank teams might be formed should that objective be considered worth pursuing.

1. One useful lead on the possible construction of Apollo *companies* came from the experience of allowing members to form a team of their own design. This occurred at a stage in the work when members had been given some practical guides on the principles of team composition as a result of the research. The procedure was that representatives from the syndicates would then meet to nominate members for one Superteam. After that we formed the remaining members into other competing *companies*. The representatives made their nominations on the basis of what they personally knew about the members and not, of course, on the basis of the test results which were not available to them. Using a strict definition of an Apollo *company* only one of the six Superteams was an Apollo and this *company* finished third. However there were three other Superteams that just fell short of our Apollo criterion of which two finished first and one third. The other two non-Apollo teams were both winners.

The members' Superteams not only achieved good results but they also succeeded in avoiding the Apollo pitfall. While the electing members took account of team-building principles, they also engaged in a number of initiatives of their own making. Superteam members were chosen for their particular skills (in numeracy, in co-ordinating ability or in control) and thereby some measure of interdependence was built up. In addition, some sophisticated thought was put into ways of correcting the imbalance in the Superteam, which those selecting it had begun to suspect might be its problem. In one instance a selector proposed somebody for the Superteam who was seen as the joker in the pack, who would take the tension out of the situation. The person he had in mind was a former Welsh international rugby forward, now of roly-poly appearance and known as a real prankster. Such foresight was rewarded exactly in the way expected. In other cases clever but very awkward members were excluded from the Superteam on the grounds that they might give more trouble than they were worth. By giving careful consideration to all the personal characteristics of members, selectors seemed capable of forming better balanced and more successful teams. These were signs that this approach could extend to Apollo and near-Apollo teams too.

2. One feature of successful Apollo teams was the absence of highly dominant individuals apart from the Chairman. The combination of a high score on the Critical Thinking Appraisal and a low score on the Assertive scale of the Personality Inventory was especially favourable. The only danger here was that such members might sit back and play a passive role unless there was someone present to pull the whole thing together.

3. Perhaps the main key to the successful Apollo team was the character of the Chairman. But the good Apollo Chairman did not behave in the same way as the Chairman of other successful teams. In Chapter Five this is discussed in some detail. Suffice it here to say that clever people seem to need leadership of a different style and type from people who are not so gifted.

Although Apollo teams could turn out very well it was more usual for them to yield disappointing results. Outcomes were always difficult to forecast since differences between success and failure depended on factors that were often no more than marginal. Apollo *companies* usually had all the talent, at least in a technical sense, that was needed if only they knew how to use it.

EXPLANATIONS OF RESULTS

Let us consider in more detail why the general run of Apollo *companies* performed so indifferently.

The first explanation is that all members of an Apollo *company* are inclined to have the same aspirations – that is to apply their critical minds to the most difficult and intellectually enticing parts of the exercise. This is borne out by the high scores which the observers recorded in these *companies* for those items of behaviour covered in "proposing" and "opposing". The emphasis was on analysis and counter-analysis. Certainly these are very important aspects of a team's activities, when faced with a set of interlocking problems; but there are other aspects that are equally important and which may be neglected. Using resources, collecting and exchanging information, recording what is known, co-ordinating plans and action all have a vital part to play in helping to make a team effective.

Some may argue that this explanation is no explanation. Why should Apollo members restrict their behaviour in this way? Why should they limit their role more than members of other *companies*? A possible answer lies in the very pressures which our educational system and culture exert on clever people. Those who at school are "top of the class", or who have it within their reach, are continually being judged in terms of their scholastic pre-eminence. To come second is to fail. Beating the next man is the name of the game. Difficult problems excite the greatest rivalry and so destroy the bonds of mutual co-operation and complementary functioning upon which the success of a team ultimately depends. In other words, overconcentration on coming top of the class provides an unconscious training in anti-teamwork.

There is another by-product of intellectual sharpness which may also cause difficulties for teams and provide therefore a second explanation of the factors underlying Apollo misfortunes. Membership of Apollo *companies* was contingent on securing a high score on the Critical Thinking Appraisal. The word "critical", as applied to the mind, has two meanings in the English language. One meaning denotes mental acumen or analytical powers. The second meaning implies a negative evaluation: a critical mind aims to find fault in another's argument or to look for and perceive shortcomings and blemishes.

High critical thinkers, we were to learn, tended to have critical minds in both senses of the word. The negative side of their perceptions was indicated by a characteristic of their scores on the test which we developed at Cambridge called the PPQ (see Glossary). The PPQ marking procedure allows for a ratio of positive and negative constructs to be scored for each respondent. In the event, high critical thinkers (as judged on the CTA) were found to have a high negative construct ratio (as judged on the PPQ). In other words clever people were finding more negative things to say about the world at large, so making them appear to have a negative outlook.

Do negative constructs mean a negative approach? Not necessarily. Negative constructs can be part of discrimination. To arrive at a worthwhile decision it may be a useful tactic to consider and dispose of all unwanted alternatives. A high proportion of negative constructs may, however, have a damaging effect on social intercourse and interfere with good team integration.

THE APOLLO SYNDROME IN PRACTICE

Once we had fully explored Apollo phenomena in the Henley management game and in Teamopoly, we began to look around for counterparts in the broader world. The most likely places in which to encounter Apollo groups are areas where clever people congregate. High-technology groups which need to recruit well-qualified and able individuals, the boards of companies which place great faith in rapid promotion on the basis of performance, and specially convened committees and working groups whose members are selected for their creative ability and expertise are just the places where one might expect difficulty. Difficulties akin to those reported in our experiments were reported to us as being very prevalent in hospital management. The key figures in hospitals are consultants and no major decisions can be made without their involvement. Meetings of hospital consultants have a certain notoriety for their failure to move smoothly to rational decisions in spite of the undoubted talents of their members. One well-informed source considers that the resulting problem underlies the tendency of the National Health Service to overreact by recruiting too many administrators!

It is difficult to assess whether a firm is likely to be prone to the Apollo syndrome without having hard data on the mental abilities of senior managers and directors. This is not easily obtained. Those in high office are often enthusiastic about administering tests, including intelligence tests, to those they are considering recruiting but they are less than enthusiastic about taking the same tests themselves. Inevitably, therefore, we are left to infer rather more than we would like about the individual abilities of members of teams observed in the industrial and commercial world.

There are two areas of industry where high mental ability is considered ahead of any of the other personal characteristics that recommend candidates for responsible appointments: one of these lies in computer applications and the other in the field of research and development.

As it happened my colleague, Roger Mottram, and I both found ourselves engaged in examining team-building problems in each of these areas soon after we had discovered the Apollo syndrome, he looking at the computer field while I concentrated on research and development. The small teams which Mottram studied operated within a large firm engaged in installing computer hardware and systems for customers. He tested the members of these teams and found the majority of them to be high critical thinkers. Some of the cleverest teams turned out to be the least successful – especially where the project manager was himself the cleverest and most creative member. It was at the level of communication that these project teams were often most vulnerable: communications were poor both within the team and with clients. Rearrangement of the teams so that a more managerial but less creative member acted as project leader was associated with a considerable gain in team effectiveness without any loss of the technical and creative capability of the team as a whole.

Experience with firms that invest heavily in research and development has added to our understanding of Apollo phenomena in terms of what can go wrong. Teams containing the cleverest members show remarkable resistance to any form of imposed organization. Exactly why this should be so is not clear. We did not notice any such tendency during our experimental work but then there were no organizational pressures imposed from outside. The nearest parallel was the tendency to disorganization evident within the team. Two instances illustrate the liking of Apollo-type teams for socially satisfying but anarchic autonomy.

A firm specializing in contract research and development and known to be the largest of its kind in the UK made every effort (with the use of tests) to recruit very clever research scientists. The policy was well rewarded and the firm prospered. At first, organization was no problem. Everyone gave a hand in whatever way was most fitting to deal with the small but steady stream of contracts that came in. Income and expenditure were balanced in the most informal way. As these scientists were mainly interested in their work, questions of relating extrinsic rewards to contribution scarcely claimed their attention. It was not a problem when everyone lent a hand to make a success of a project. But as more research contracts were placed the scientists needed to divide their responsibilities in a more equitable fashion so that each took the work most appropriate to his particular skills and abilities. Some projects went better than others and in the case of fixed price contracts it became clear that the company was making a good deal of profit on some contracts while losing money on projects giving difficulty. The stage had now been reached when some administrative function was needed at managerial level if the company was to meet its commitments, make a profit, and prosper generally. All recognized this. All recognized also that such work was not to their liking and that an entirely different species of human being was required to cope with the work envisaged. In due course the company found an appropriate manager with the requisite experience and personal qualities. The new manager soon got down to work drawing up forms upon which essential information could be gathered for the purpose of financial control. To enable the company to quote a price for a contract more accurately than it had done in the past, a record was needed of the number of hours that each scientist devoted to each project. The minutes were immaterial. Even a global estimate of the hours spent on projects would furnish the controllers with all the information required to improve the company's profitability.

The system never worked. It failed at the start. Creative scientists did not see themselves wasting their valuable time filling in forms. Worse, they began to develop some antagonism to the petty-minded manager, as they saw him, who demanded the information. Filled with frustration the manager left. The company now regressed to its blissful bohemian existence only to run deeper into the problems which had called for such an appointment in the first place. This time it was resolved that an appointment should be made of a manager who was a scientist rather than a professional administrator, but a scientist with a flair for organization. Eventually a very interesting candidate was found with a particular interest in the commercial side of operations. This man seemed to have everything that was needed and he soon found himself prominently placed near the apex of the company. Unfortunately, as his influence grew and even as the company found its trading position improving, a cleavage began to develop and then widen between this organization man and the original boffins who had made the company what it was. The point was reached when the manager began to feel that life could be more comfortable in another company. A new opportunity beckoned and the company was left once again in its primeval state.

The second example deals with a manufacturing company with a very heavy expenditure in research and development. Long-established and more traditional companies develop a culture in which the needs for systems and organization are appreciated and those who run them have a certain social standing. What happens then when an Apollo group forms in such a company?

> This large company was separated into a number of semi-autonomous divisions, each of which maintained its own research and development effort, while at the same time drawing on a corporate laboratory. In one of the divisions with a particularly heavy R. and D. budget there emerged a scientist with such a breadth of talent that he soon found himself figuring prominently in all those wider, more managerial questions, with which a research department ultimately becomes embroiled. At the same time there was about him a touch of the maverick. Such a man is almost safer occupying a position of responsibility than criticizing play from the sidelines. In due course after he had reached as high a position in the hierarchy as he could without removing the current incumbents, it was realized that some career path would have to be made for him, either within the division or in the company as a whole. He was young enough to consider an appointment outside research; but on the other hand, his seniority made it difficult to find the appropriate slot. In career terms, what he now needed was to be given his head in a position of greater responsibility than that which he had already held.
>
> After a short absence from the company, I returned to inquire what had happened to our friend. Yes, he had gone from the research department. An appointment had been found for him at the company's corporate laboratory. His scientific experience was too valuable to lose, yet he needed fresh fields to conquer. Naturally one was interested to learn more about the position he had taken up. The answer came as something of a surprise. "He will be a senior man at the corporate laboratory working with the research manager. The deputy research manager? No, not exactly. By that I don't mean he won't be the deputy research manager. He will be but he mustn't be called it. You see the scientists there recognize the authority of the research manager but they will not recognize the authority of anyone under him. It makes it difficult. Someone has to do the job but without having the benefit of the title."

Why should Apollo members get into such a tizzy about authority, management, leadership and organization? One can think of no fundamental personality reasons why this should be so. Examination of the test scores of high critical thinkers showed that they came in all shapes and sizes: introverted, extroverted, dominant, recessive, anxious, stable and so on.

INTERACTION IN APOLLO TEAMS

One possibility arises from the difficulties caused by the tendency of clever people to overvalue cleverness. High scorers on the CTA showed a marked inclination to be strongly influenced by "brain" constructs on the PPQ especially negative brain constructs: in other words those with high mental ability showed both that they admired intelligence and that they did not suffer fools gladly. This respect and need for other clever people like themselves can create difficulty. If they find the colleagues they are seeking, they are likely to find themselves making similar and therefore competing contributions. This easily leads to a loss in role identity and so to role confusion. The question of leadership aggravates the problem. To the high critical thinker, with his outlook governed by "brain" constructs, leadership is often taken to mean the ability to analyse the problem and point to the solution. In the eyes of rank-and-file but clever members of a team, there is little distinction between what they see as their role and what they see as the leader's role.

The manager's concept of his own responsibility for making decisions directly conflicts, or is capable of doing so, with the cleverest member's natural aptitude for evaluating problems. Managers are probably more concerned with synthesis than analysis. They are often supplied with a great deal of pre-analysed material; their function is to make a balanced decision having regard to all factors in a situation, including human factors. A manager needs a fair measure of mental ability but that may not be the most important requirement for his job.

If Apollo members find themselves competing for some aspects of the leadership role without being able to discharge that role in its broader sense, they are likely to disrupt rather than contribute to the effective functioning of the group. The points at issue they raise will not be readily resolved. Debating skills do not bind people together. If anything they cause and open up rifts and divisions.

We may sum up by reflecting on what has been observed. The Apollo syndrome refers to a phenomenon found in groups whose members are chosen primarily for their critical thinking faculties whereby destructive tendencies come to the fore and result in an underachievement by the team as a whole. People with high analytical abilities are not necessarily creative. High mental ability does however imply some ability to produce ideas.

Good ideas take time to develop. They demand favourable conditions. There may be men with ideas in an Apollo company but the Apollo company is not the place where a person gifted with creative ability is likely to flourish.

An Apollo team is not therefore in any effective sense a creative team.

3: Teams Containing Similar Personalities

The tests used in our experiments enabled us to look at members of teams along various dimensions of personality and to use these variables as the primary basis for forming teams of people with particular characteristics. If the general level of mental ability was not the decisive advantage in the EME that might have been supposed, then certain factors of character, that are easily neglected because they are more difficult to assess, might turn out to be more important. Experiments were now planned with teams of members with similar personality characteristics.

REASONS FOR EXPERIMENTS

The business of allocating managers to particular teams on the basis of their scores on measures of personality is of theoretical interest but is not just a theoretical exercise. Individuals with particular personality characteristics tend to be drawn towards particular occupations. If they rise in these areas into positions of responsibility in management, then members of these management teams are likely to have much in common. The tendency is furthered by what might be called the principle of elective homogeneity. This refers to some group of related factors that cause firms to recruit a particular type of person. One aspect of this is the natural tendency for managers to recruit in their own image. Fat and jolly managers are apt to see fatness and jollity as an essential part of management, just as wiry, sober managers see their own cerebral kind as an essential for the effective operation of the firm. This tendency is compounded by a second and perhaps more important force. The culture of any employing body tends to favour a particular type of personality. There are forms of behaviour that attract acceptance and prestige in one organization that might repel in another. People are often aware that these are very subtle and are difficult to put down on paper. Nevertheless most of those responsible for recruiting share a common image of the sort of man they think would fit in. This phenomenon is discussed in more detail on pp. 83–5.

So strong is the pressure to recruit a person who fits into the standard mould that some managers react against this by being deliberately casual about the methods they use in recruitment. The argument is that there is room in a firm for all types of people; that even those with unusual idiosyncrasies will find their role somewhere within the organization. The only proviso is that they are technically competent in the area for which they are being recruited.

PERSONALITY TYPES AND OCCUPATION

The personality measures we employed gave us a closer insight into the make-up of managers participating in the experiments and enabled us to classify them according to various basic types (see diagram on p. 23). The two well-researched scales of introversion and anxiety/stability produced four broad types which are also associated with well-known executive occupations.

> Stable Extroverts are known to fulfil themselves and excel in jobs which place a premium on liaison work and where co-operation is sought from others. They flourish as sales representatives and do well in personnel management.
>
> Anxious Extroverts are commonly found where people need to work at a high pace and exert pressure on others. Anxious Extroversion seems to confer an occupational advantage among sales managers, works managers, and editors.
>
> Stable Introverts seem to do well in work where good relationships with a small number of people need to be maintained over a period. They flourish as administrators, solicitors, local and central government officials, and in industry, as corporate planners.
>
> Anxious Introverts distinguish themselves in jobs which call for self-direction and self-sustaining persistence. They predominate among research scientists and among specialists committed to long-term assignments. Some of the most creative people belong to this group.

Individuals within any one occupational grouping naturally vary in personality. Nevertheless the deliberate creation of homogeneity in a management team had the effect of unbalancing the occupational breakdown of the teams we composed. Stable Extrovert teams contained, as expected, an undue proportion of people in Sales, Marketing and Personnel: they were often short of members with skills in numeracy and we could seldom find members in Engineering or Research and Development functions who could be put into the team. For Anxious Introvert teams we found quite a few eligible accountants to add to the expected quota of research men and miscellaneous boffins. The difficulty now was that the AI teams tended to have a superfluity of numerate personnel.

Teams of Anxious Extroverts and Stable Introverts also had their own distinctive characteristics. AE teams were not difficult to form, for we were supplied with a good cross-section of managers covering a wide range of functions; but well to the fore were General Managers, followed by Managers of Management Services and a sprinkling of Bankers. For some reason, however, there was an insufficiency of members suitable for SI teams. The lack of Stable Introverts on courses being run for senior managers may suggest that not many Stable Introverts progress into the higher echelons of management. Or it could be that they keep away from management courses. These two possibilities are not mutually exclusive. It is a fair guess that pure SIs, though very employable and efficient in a functional sense, are prone to passivity and overcontentment. This could reduce their sense of need to develop themselves through further education in management and also lessen the likelihood of their reaching top positions. The exceptions we came across were individuals with very high scores in mental ability. These managers did not have the typical managerial temperament or the need for achievement but they did seem actuated by a sense of intellectual quest and inquiry. As managers they made their mark as strategic thinkers.

Although our teams of SEs, AEs, SIs, and AIs were not then perfectly matched in occupational background or mental ability, they had a distinctive flavour of their own which seemed to emerge irrespective of the different contexts and demands of the EME and Teamopoly and the different sources of information by means of which we learned about their characters. In the case of the EME we had independent observer notes and reports, sometimes copious, to guide us, while for Teamopoly we had to rely on our own observations supplemented by the reports from the members of the *companies* themselves at the public inquest on the final day. In this latter case members engaged in this self-revelation were remarkably perceptive about themselves and their colleagues, often hilariously so. From these observations a picture began to emerge of the typical styles of work which our four sets of *companies* were prone to adopt.

PURE TEAMS – THEIR SUCCESSES AND FAILURES

Extroverted *companies* tended to perform better than introverted. The SE *companies* did well in the EME (*see* Chapter Eight). The differences between the other three *companies* were small. The AEs were marginally better than the SIs, while the AIs were rather prone to be the bottom markers. Where they did achieve an above average result this was usually due to the performance of one star member. In Teamopoly AEs were more successful than the SEs while both teams tended to have the upper hand over the SIs and the AIs.

While we could attribute some difference in the merit order of the "pure" teams as between the EME and Teamopoly to the varying demands of the two exercises, some additional factors emerged as important. In the case of Teamopoly the eventual outcome depended on the way in which the game was managed. The pace could be slowed or it could be quickened. Crises could be averted or induced and allowed to multiply. All this was rendered possible by control over the timing of those external events which generated the pressures. On the whole the provision of a longer unfilled (i.e. crisis free) period favoured the introverted teams since they displayed more readiness to put that time to good effect. But the reactions depended on the exact circumstances.

A long interval before some critical point in the game tended to produce problems for two opposite types of team: the SEs and the AIs. The SEs found it difficult to concentrate when presented with a long, event-free period. In one Teamopoly venue in Australia, we chose a location for the exercise that had a snooker table at one end of a large room we were using. The SE team selected for their *company* site a side room very near the snooker table and its members were unable to resist the temptation of taking pot shots at snooker when they should have been using the time more properly for planning. AIs on the other hand were inclined to take their initial planning sessions so seriously that they had difficulty in extricating themselves from a compulsive fixation on decision-making dilemmas. In another seminar in Australia where prolonged time was given for the initial decision–what strategy to adopt at the initial auction and the initial tender–an AI *company* became so engrossed with the complications that they succeeded in missing both auction and tender.

Teamopoly

A long event-free period after a *company* had experienced its first crisis or reverse usually operated more to the advantage of introverted teams and rather less to the benefit of extroverted teams. SE teams tended to

EXPERIMENTS WITH "PURE" TEAMS

Performance Characteristics

Stable extrovert teams

Pull well together; enjoy group work; versatile approach; use resources well but inclined to be euphoric and lazy.
Results: good on the whole, but individually rather dependent on one another and on others.

Anxious extrovert teams

Dynamic, entrepreneurial; good at seizing opportunities; prone to healthy altercation; easily distracted and liable to rush off at tangents.
Results: good in rapidly changing situations but unreliable in performance at other times.

Stable introvert teams

Plan well; strong in organization; but slow-moving and liable to neglect new factors in a situation.
Results: generally indifferent

Anxious introvert teams

Capable of good ideas but a tendency to be preoccupied; lacking cohesion as a team.
Results: usually poor

shrug off their misfortune. Their ability to keep smiling allowed them to focus their attention on the possibilities ahead, and to discount recent adverse experience and also any general lessons it carried. AI teams, on the other hand, never failed to take note that a setback had something to teach. The AI team which had missed the first auction and tender thereafter became the most punctilious *company* on timing, detail, and anything that called for precision. Introverted *companies* in Teamopoly were often poor starters in exploiting negotiating opportunities; but they were ready to change their policy towards negotiation provided they were given long enough time to think about it. They would then become committed negotiators, even if their skills in this area were undistinguished.

Teamopoly also gave the umpire a chance to bring in events that had the effect of creating momentary crises. The compulsory purchase of undeveloped property, allowed for in the rules, or the staging of simultaneous events that tended to interfere with company organization and the efficient use of resources disrupted introverted companies more than extroverted ones. Here the greatest contrast was provided between AE and SI companies.

AE teams often behaved as though operating in a permanent state of bedlam. When the objective conditions of the exercise added to the natural state of bedlam AE members responded with vigour and enthusiasm. They showed little inhibition in making on-the-spot decisions in an individual way, and then sorting out all the inconsistencies and contradictions afterwards. Arguments, accusations, and counter-accusations abounded. These were less destructive than they might appear, for they served to bring out the crunch issues which were to have an important bearing on the ultimate result. In contrast, some *companies* never got to grips with the issues that mattered: they enjoyed peace and harmony but not success.

At the other end of the psychological spectrum were the SIs. These *companies* were immune to disruption, or so it seemed, plodding on with their basic strategies as though new experiences and data produced no real need for strategy revision. Without the self-doubts of the AIs or the outward-looking negotiating tendencies of the SEs, they were marked by a certain consistency of effort and approach. Occasionally this consistency was rewarded, especially where some critical success had been gained on which they could capitalize.

Whether a team with a certain type of member achieves good or poor results depends on the characteristic opportunity setting in which the team finds itself. That is why the attributes of teams always have to be assessed against the demands and possibilities of the situation. There were opportunities for each type of pure team in the differing conditions and circumstances which the two exercises provided.

The EME differed from Teamopoly in requiring a higher measure of analysis, calculation, recording, and scientifically based strategy-making, necessitating a good deal of close co-ordination, and in this respect was typical of the business game. Teamopoly, on the other hand, was akin more to a commercial business enterprise, with ideas, entre-preneurial flair and negotiating skill laying the foundations for success.

A Closer Look at the Stable Extrovert Team

Since the SEs were the most successful of the four groups in the EME, it is worth studying how they tended to operate and achieve their results. The categories of behaviour recorded by observers showed that, relative to other *companies*, *proposing* was at a fairly high level, *opposing* at a low level, and *commenting* at a very high level. The typical picture was of a chatterbox company whose members co-operated well with one another and stimulated each other into ideas. The other three pure *companies* did not show any particular characteristic patterns.

Detailed examination of the records showed that SE *companies* derived an advantage from the superior use they made of both internal and external communications. Their operational style within the *company* usually followed one of two patterns. The first was characterized by a great deal of collective work. Important issues were treated comprehensively by allowing for the expression of each departmental standpoint. This reduced the amount of time available for the detailed work that fell within the responsibility of individual members. In compensation, major mistakes were avoided and progress broadly followed the right lines. This propensity towards collective work was not shared by the other *companies*.

The second pattern entailed a greater measure of direct responsibility; but here instead of working in isolation, members of SE *companies* tended to work in pairs. This meant that no major decision ever depended on any single person. The pairing itself operated in a flexible way. Occasionally a member would join another pair or pairs would swap partners. Such exchanges made it very difficult for our observers to follow what was going on. What can be said in general terms is that SE *companies* in one way or another found favourable means of developing their systems of internal communication.

Perhaps the main prowess of SE *companies*, however, lay in their ability to make good use of external resources. In the EME there were several ways in which this could be done. The *companies* could make use of banks during the cash flow crisis that usually appeared somewhere in the middle of the exercise. One SE *company* sent a member along to chat up the banker at a time when it had no borrowing requirement. Later the contact established helped the *company* to raise money on favourable terms. Other *companies* objected to this "unfair treatment" but the banker retorted, not unreasonably, that he preferred dealing with people he knew. The SEs also did well in dealing with "trade unions" when in recent years these were introduced into the EME. Early discussions were arranged and strike-free agreements were entered into well in advance of the pressures which adverse trading conditions produced for employee relationships. Yet another resource that SE *companies* used to advantage was the record sheets produced by the observers. The observers were under instruction neither to volunteer the information they were collecting nor to keep it back if people wanted to see it. SE companies often took an interest in what was going on, with the result that *company* style was sometimes modified so as to make it more effective. Perhaps the most striking use of resources, however, was illustrated by the response of an SE *company* to the possibility of using an operational research consultant.

Tom Child, seconded to the College on a research project, had a specialized knowledge of mathematical models as they affect business operations. It seemed quite appropriate that he should be available as a resource during the EME. At the same time it was agreed with the organizers that he would not be allowed to solve personally any problems that a *company* in' the exercise brought to the fore. Accordingly, the consultant did his rounds at the start of one exercise, explaining what help he might offer. The reception he received was something less than warm. The equivocal nature of his help as a consultant was seen by some *companies* as being irritating. Tom was referred to as highhanded and aggravating; and other less than complimentary words were registered by the observers as being applied to him by aggrieved interviewers.

The SEs' reaction to Tom Child was of a different order. He was received by the *company* as a whole and after various questions had been posed and answers given, it was agreed that one of their number should keep in contact with him. Tom responded to what seemed to him a cordial reception in a positive fashion. While the help given to this *company* remained indirect, the hints, clues and leads offered turned out to be ample reward for the patience expended. The SE *company* cheerfully modified its policy—without quite fully understanding what it was doing—and was delighted to find its fortunes bound upwards to give it the lead in financial performance. It was a lead they failed to consolidate but by the final session they were still strongly placed.

LESSONS OF RESULTS

The four *pure companies* we have been considering all had merits which gave them advantages in particular situations. But they were also susceptible to particular weaknesses. Our SE companies, for example, were prone to make small errors which in their easy-going way they failed to note or rectify. Because the members of these companies had much in common, the natural balancing qualities found in groups with diverse members were absent. Nevertheless groups with similar types of members are usually able to find a style of operation which suits all the members.

It may be argued that in the industrial and commercial world pure companies never exist. Even if a company wished to recruit in its own image, it would have difficulty in doing so since chance factors bring forward all manner of people eligible for the vacancies that arise. Against this is a view that some firms cultivate a culture that is close to one of the four basic personality types and that such a culture exercises an overriding effect on personal behaviour, at least in so far as it is expressed within the firm. For example, parallels have been drawn between the typical AE *companies* as observed in our experiments and certain newspaper groups in the publishing world. In the same way SI cultures are found in local government, and AI cultures in research. As it happens, individuals belonging to these organizations commonly fit into the personality pattern that might be naturally expected from them. However this is not always so. Inevitably a certain amount of misfit does occur. In these cases behaviour within the organization is more likely to accord with the "personality" of the culture than with the natural personality of the individual. In this respect so-called national characteristics should not be dismissed as stereotypes, for they reflect the culture of which the stereotype is itself a product.

This point is well brought out by multinational companies. The value of such companies is that they can transport a culture overseas, assimilating foreign nationals in the process and so maintaining the impetus and dynamism of the parent. Naturally this very strength is a source of the resentment which multinationals attract. What is forgotten is that the culture lies at the very heart of what a company is able to achieve.

A good example of a thriving SE company in a foreign land is Mars Ltd. and its subsidiary, Petfoods Ltd. Mars is a privately owned American company with a larger turnover in the UK than in the USA. The employees of Mars are highly paid and there are no trade unions. When Mars was set up on the Slough Trading Estate its style created something of a cultural shock. It was as though it had been deliberately designed to counter the insularity of managers and the loss of communication which excessive social stratification engenders in traditionally run English firms. Offices were organized on an open plan; managers and workers used the same canteen. An employee could walk into the personnel manager's office at any time to air a grievance. Coats were taken off when discussions took place. Christian names were prevalent. Open management, free communications and buddy relationships were fostered. The culture has also influenced the selection process. Graduates are expected to perform well in group discussion and generally to show strong ability in the capacity to communicate. Those who are recruited to Mars may not all be SEs but if they behave like SEs they are likely to contribute to the continued progress of the firm along lines that are already proven.

The pure types of *company* which formed the design basis of our experimental management teams were chosen because these parameters of behaviour were measurable, with tests, and were already known to have an important bearing on performance. There was no reason for presuming, however, that a choice had to be made from among these team types. There were perhaps other team types that could prove more effective and interesting. This was the more worth exploring as there were many members who could not be fitted into one of the *pure companies*, because they themselves did not conform to any one type.

PERSONALITY AND THE EFFECTIVE TEAM MEMBER

We looked next to see if we could identify a team member common to successful teams. The approach was to examine the 16PF test scores (see Glossary) of members of teams that had gained good results in the EME and to compare them with the scores of those belonging to *companies* that had suffered poor financial results. Isolating those factors that were the best differentiators, we grouped them into a cluster to give us the type we were looking for. We needed a name for this type; we called him a Company Worker. The choice of the name reflected the factors that were revealed.

Six factors were involved. The CW was a disciplined individual. Conscientious and aware of external obligations, he also had a well-developed sense of self-image giving him a degree of internal control. He was tough-minded (the strongest sex differentiator in the test, here giving him a strong masculine characteristic), practical, trusting, tolerant towards others, and finally conservative in the sense of being a respecter of established conditions and ways of looking at things.

Introversion/extroversion together with anxiety/stability use up between them ten of the sixteen factors. CW characteristics incorporated only two of the ten. Both of these were associated with low anxiety – the trusting tolerant quality, and the controlled self-image, with its associated lack of self-conflict.

Once the CW cluster had been isolated, the scene was set for an experiment in validation. During a period of two years *companies* competing in the EME were composed according to their CW characteristics. There were pure *companies* high in CW and there were pure *companies* low in CW. Mental ability was also controlled in case this proved a decisive factor conditioning effectiveness. There were therefore CW *companies* high in mental ability and CW *companies* low in mental ability.

LIMITATIONS OF PURE CW TEAMS

We expected some interesting results from these experiments but the results were largely negative. If CW members were associated with good team results, then pure *companies*, full of CW men, failed to produce better results than average, even in association with high mental ability. In later years we tried pure CW *companies* in Teamopoly and the picture was very similar.

Although our results were negative, the experiments were not deemed a failure. Our good fortune in having a few excellent observers over this period gave us a lead in the shortcomings of the pure CW *company*. The CW man, as we have seen, was a well-organized, disciplined but tolerant, practical and rather orthodox person. He accepted the constraints of the game and applied himself unquestioningly to what was required. He was therefore an asset to a company that was taking the exercise seriously and trying to win.

Collectively however CWs did not produce good teams. Observer scores and comments presented a picture of organization and effort but of a lack of real ideas. CW teams were also found to be prone to inflexibility once they had established their frame of reference. They were strongly committed to anything they set in motion and were disturbed by having to change plans. They worked well but failed to get good results.

The experience with CW *companies* brought to the fore the limitations of *pure* teams. Pure teams develop a style and quality of their own. If the situation matches that style the pure company can excel. In practice there can be no guarantee that any particular situation or demand will continue in a given form. The longer a management team is exposed to the problems of the real world the greater is the need to be prepared for a full range of problems and situations, and to have the resources in a team ready to meet them.

What does emerge from the experiments described in this chapter is that teams of similar people have characteristic strengths and weaknesses. The question we will need to carry forward is, how can the strengths be retained and the weaknesses eliminated?

4:   Creativity In The Team

Most large organizations are interested in the forming of creative teams. The favoured approach is to take an already existing team and to make it more creative than it would otherwise tend to be. "Brainstorming" pioneered this field and later "synectics" and "lateral thinking" added to the repertoire of means available for encouraging a flow of ideas directed towards the solving of problems. There is no doubt that the tools now exist for enabling groups to generate ideas and ideas in quantity. Where groups look prone to the overcritical proclivities of the Apollo syndrome these methods have much to recommend them.

To what extent can a prolific flow of ideas be taken as the hallmark of the creative group? For a long time it seemed a reasonable bet that one was a fair indicator of the other. Not only does a creative group need an adequate range of ideas, but the more the members of a group contribute to their production, the greater the sense of personal involvement and identification with the object of the proceedings.

The first glimmerings of doubt about the merits of this approach began to dawn on us after close examination of the observer records. It was true that some teams were held back by their inability to generate an adequate number of ideas. But with these exceptions there was not the slightest tendency for greater success in the EME to go with a higher count on proposing. In fact some of its most successful teams had a below average count on this score: they seemed well able to elicit a few good suggestions and to act on them appropriately.

This prompted us to look around industry to assess how effective were those groups that were being consciously moulded to make them "creative". What we thought we saw was the recurring phenomenon of a lack of ability to utilize the ideas produced. Working from the other direction, we looked at cases where important "breakthroughs" had actually been made. What struck us in these instances was the basic simplicity of the social process. With the right combination of people the act of creation seemed effortless.

MAKING USE OF CREATIVE ABILITY IN A TEAM

With the benefit this insight rendered by combining experimental and industrial experiences, we began to develop some different hypotheses about the conditions which bring about creativity in the team. We could now see obvious drawbacks in encouraging everyone in a group to become creative. There is the problem of disposing of unwanted ideas, which is part of the process of eventual arrival at those one or two ideas that are worth adopting. In practice, the most politically acceptable way of narrowing down the choices is to combine the ideas of the most dominant members. The search for compromise can soon become a matter of appeasement with technical objections to combining proposals that may be incompatible taking second place. As a way out of this danger some people advocate setting up two teams, one to generate ideas and the other to evaluate them. This suggestion has merits but for everyday purposes seems somewhat complicated.

The alternative strategy to encouraging all the members of a group to engage in the identical task of producing ideas (a somewhat wasteful use of manpower) is to induce a team to understand and to make better use of the individual talents of its members. Some individuals are gifted with a truly innovative turn of mind. If that talent can be recognized and harnessed, the "noise" problem is avoided. There is no need to sift through all the ideas that can be produced. One original "spark" can set off a new line of thought in the development of which all may find a part to play. A simple decision can then be made as to whether the resultant package is sound or not and that can become the responsibility of a person of mature judgement.

Identifying Creative Potential

We now run into the problem of being able to identify this specialist idea-maker in the first place. In the EME the observer records showed which members had engaged in most proposing, but there was no way of knowing how good any of these proposals were. We had set in motion a system for recording which proposals were acted upon and which were ignored, whereby individuals whose ideas had proved the most productive could be traced. Unfortunately, some of our observers found themselves unable to use the method, especially when discussions lost any semblance of control or direction. As a standard method it had to be abandoned. However we did glean enough information before this happened to find a relationship between the most prolific idea-makers and the ideas that were used. The relationship suggested that we would not be too far out if we regarded the leading *proposing* rates as belonging to the most creative members.

In this way a sample was formed of people with probable creative tendencies. Their test records were then examined. We duly isolated a cluster of distinguishing characteristics only to find that the treasure trove had already been discovered by a previous explorer. Our cluster was none other than the pre-existing Cattell formula for Creative Disposition (CD). From then onwards the CD formula was to become a valuable tool for identifying creative individuals. We adopted it as it stood, as the means of ensuring that any team we were to compose had some creative potential within it.

For those readers unfamiliar with the name of Cattell, a few words of introduction may be timely. Raymond Cattell was born in Staffordshire in 1905 and retired in 1973 at the University of Illinois, where he was research professor in psychology and director of the Laboratory of Personality and Group Behaviour Research. Cattell received all his education in England, gaining from the University of London a BSc in Chemistry and a PhD in Psychology, later followed by a DSc in recognition of his wide scientific work. But most of his work for which he is best known was conducted in the United States culminating in the award of the Wenner-Gren prize by the New York Academy of Science. While his name is closely associated with the dozen intelligence, personality, and clinical tests that bear his name, Cattell's written output, prior to his retirement (and there have been no signs of slackening) included twenty-two books and monographs and 235 scientific articles.

The Cattell Personality Inventory (16PF) has probably been more researched into, in terms of its bearing on industrial occupation categories, than any other personality measure. As far as creativity was concerned Cattell's method was to obtain a large number of nominations of people considered creative in their particular fields, ranging over the arts and the sciences. He managed to persuade these nominees to take his personality inventory and then compared their test scores with those of the general population. They differed from the general population on ten of the sixteen scales with the highest

NOTES ON FACES

Each face represents a *Company* in the EME where five or six members have similar scores on the psychometric tests. The sixth or seventh member is a Plant.

Explanation of Symbols

The nature of the face and clothing indicates the characteristics of the Company

Round Face   = High Extrovert
Smile   = Low Anxiety
Frown   = High Anxiety
Mortar Board = Clever
Dunce Cap   = No one clever except for Plant
Collar and Tie = "Company Worker"
Artist's Smock = Some Plant-like Characteristics

Figures floating in the air refer to characteristics of Plants

Star   = Very creative disposition (a superplant
                 characteristic)
Mortar Board = Very clever (a superplant characteristic)
Collar and Tie = "Company Worker" Plant
Halo   = Plant relating very well with Chairman
Dagger   = Plant clashing with Chairman

Half-Pie Chart
Black Pie   = % proposals of Plant where half a pie represents 50%
                 of all proposals in *company*.

= Expected contribution for seven-member *companies*
  I,N,P,X

= Expected contribution for six-member *companies*

RESULTS OF ONE YEAR'S EXPERIMENTATION

Creative individuals were "planted" into "pure" *companies*, one per *company*.
Note: Plants tend to flower (have a relatively high proposal rate) or otherwise fail to flower.

How did these *companies* differ in what they achieved? For the rank order of *company* success turn to p. 159, and read in association with Chapters Seven and Eight.

PLANTS' SHARES OF PROPOSALS IN DIFFERENT TYPES OF *COMPANY*

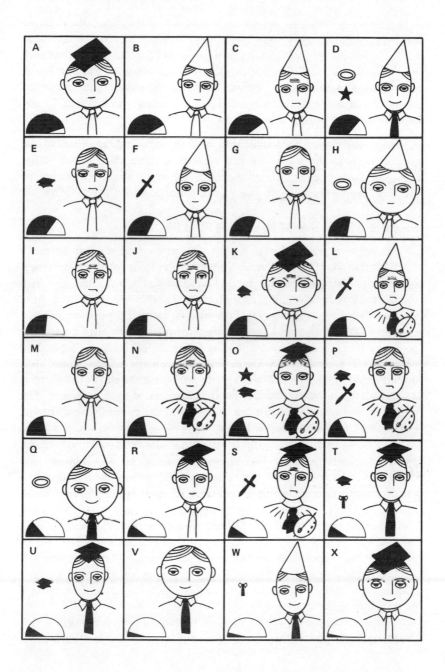

weightings on intelligence, tender-mindedness, and three of the scales belonging to introversion. The creative were also more dominant, socially bold, natural, imaginative and radical.

Before we attempt to construct a picture of the typically creative individual from his test scores, it is as well to reflect on one fundamental matter. Creative ability is usually thought of as being linked in some way with measurable intelligence. Cattell's formula contains the link but it establishes something more: a creative individual has a distinctive set of personal qualities that lie embedded in his character and which do not depend on intelligence.

Although the Cattell formula fitted well the data on individuals who created ideas in the teams we had observed, there seemed a case for cross-validating the formula on the teams we were about to construct, in this case testing the accuracy of our experience-based predictions.

EXPERIMENTS WITH CREATIVITY

So we began a series of experiments the aim of which was to make predictions about the creative abilities of individuals with particular sets of scores on the psychometric tests. The form was to pick out those with the highest combination of scores on mental ability – in this instance the Critical Thinking Appraisal (CTA)–and Creative Disposition (on the Cattell CD formula) and to plant each high scorer into a separate *company* where his behaviour could be recorded by an independent observer. The observer, who had no knowledge of the hypothesis underlying the experiments, was able to provide at the end of the exercise a total score on Proposing for the six members of each *company*. The scores could be arranged in rank order from the person who did most Proposing to the one who did least.

The key individual, with the most potentially creative profile in the psychometric tests, we called the Plant, since he was planted for experimental purposes into the *company*. Technically we had come to the conclusion that we required a score of 80 on CTA and 98 on CD. In some cases we fell just short of these qualifying figures so that those chosen we termed Subplants. Others who were almost over-qualified became known as Superplants. At any rate we ended up with one clever person (Plant, Superplant, or Subplant) per *company*. The experimental study covered 38 *companies* with 38 chosen Plants (or their equivalents). The identity of the Plants was not disclosed to the other team members or to the observers.

The results supported the prediction. Out of the six positions in which the Plant could rank within the *company* as an idea-maker, Plants came first in thirteen cases and second in twelve cases. The corresponding figures for third, fourth, fifth and sixth places were three, one, eight and one respectively. Clearly the trend was in the expected direction.

More impressive still was the way in which Plants transformed the job assigned to them in the exercise. Jobs varied in terms of the opportunity that each provided for generating ideas. Members of *companies* who were given responsibility for Marketing produced the highest Proposing rate, followed by Chairman, and then in turn those looking after Finance, Production, and Management Services. Last was Secretary. From Marketing to Company Secretary there was a steep gradient so that the Marketing man was three times more likely to produce recorded Proposals than the Company Secretary. Plants were fairly evenly distributed amongst five of the jobs. Only in the role of Company Secretary were significantly more Plants found than we would have expected by chance.

The experience of having Plants in the Company Secretary role illustrates what happens when an individual has abilities that would not normally receive expression in a job. Several observers provided illuminating notes on this theme. One Plant Company Secretary developed the subtle ploy of producing an idea as though it were a simple elaboration of a point made by another member (which it was not), and then gaining the sanction of the *company* to record it as part of the *company* plan. One habit of the Plant Secretary was to work closely with the Chairman, acting like a faithful scribe, while at the same time taking advantage of his position in having the Chairman's ear to introduce a number of new ideas. These were later presented formally to the group for consideration and ratification by the Chairman himself. Clearly the qualities of the person can override the type of behaviour implied by the title of the job.

While we were seeking, for experimental purposes, to place one Plant into each *company* in every course, we were precluded from comparing the fortunes of *companies* possessing Plants with those lacking them. When eventually we were able to make such comparison (see Chapter Eight) the advantage to a *company* in having a Plant was well supported. However, there are limits on how far creative ability can be considered an asset. Good ideas, as we have seen, are not always well received, especially if there are too many of them. *Companies* with more than one Plant were found to fare no better than *companies* with none. Similar individual strengths offered no collective asset. The situation was comparable to that noted earlier with pure Company Worker teams and pure clever teams (Apollo groups). As in cooking, a surfeit of a needed ingredient ruins the dish.

The observers did admittedly describe some *companies* as "very creative". As the objective evidence that might have supported this was lacking, we came to the view that they were really depicting effective *companies* that knew how to take full advantage of good ideas. A creative *company* is not, any more than it is in the general business world, a pure *company* comprising people all of whom are creative.

USING INDIVIDUAL CREATIVITY

The essence of skilfully employing a Plant lay in recognizing his potential, giving him scope and a fitting role, not allowing him to pursue unrewarding lines of thought that happen to engage his fancy, and generally keeping him in his place. Whether a Plant was treated in the right way had a major bearing on the degree of success a *company* achieved. At Henley we found that such matters as recognition and treatment were much affected by the general climate prevailing in particular courses. One cannot be sure why the climate varied from one to another, but vary it did. Similar variations occurred from one *company* to another in the EME and also between *companies* in our Teamopoly exercise. Expressed in simple terms one might say that once managers attending a course or seminar came to realize the value of the Plant contribution, there was one of two possible reactions. Either a sense of emulation would develop: everyone wanted to be a Plant; or managers would become aware of the need to recognize and use Plants. It was this latter reaction that we judged to be more adaptive and which in practice yielded better *company* results.

After successfully proving – or so we thought – that Plants produce more ideas than other people, we followed up Plant behaviour in subsequent courses and detected some remarkable ways in which the proposal rate can change. For example, in two successive courses at Henley, yielding eighteen Plants, we had tried placing more than one Plant in a *company* to see what the effect would be. Three *companies* were given three Plants each and two *companies* two Plants each. Hence there were some *companies* in which it would have been physically impossible for one of the Plants to get a better ranking than third in the Proposing rate. Even so seven of the Plants finished first, four finished second and seven finished third in the rank order of Proposing in their respective *companies*. None finished fourth, fifth or sixth.

After this outstanding result the dominance of Plants in idea-making in *companies* seemed settled. But no; three other courses in combination produced a total of sixteen plants. In terms of the six ranked positions in which Plants could appear in the Proposing rate there was a completely flat spread, with two Plants coming first, two last, and three appearing in each of the intermediate positions. What had changed?

We cannot be completely sure that even now we have the answer. But these three courses were associated with a new procedure. The seven contribution categories used by observers, of which Proposing was one, were replaced with eight team-role categories of contributing. One of these was called Plant. In the event this was not such a matter of detail as it may sound. Members of *companies*, who as part of the educational process had been encouraged to use resources, soon found that something of interest, and perhaps relevance to their team functioning, could be gained by looking at the observer records. Changing the recording system made the records easier to decipher. The Plant contribution rate was one that was instantly recognizable, since the members would at an earlier stage in the course have heard about Plants in a lecture on team-building. In all this, the observer had been told to be passive. Only with such a brief could he assess the extent to which members of a *company* used resources. Non-plant members could now increase their Plant contribution rate at will. This may have satisfied their vanity but it had the inevitable effect of undermining any sensible strategy on team-building.

In general, a training course that uses team activities can adopt an appropriate or inappropriate attitude to Plants in the same way that a firm can in the real business world. It was ultimately this realization, that damage may well be done if members of a *company* misconceive what we chose to call their team-role, that led us to develop a team-role perception inventory, copies of which were handed out to members of syndicates well before the management game started. In this inventory each team-role was described together with the personal attributes of the person most likely to fit it well and members were invited to allocate ten points to each person in their syndicate. The assessment procedure was non-threatening and non-discriminatory, since each person assessed received the same number of points in total. In practice most assessors distributed their points for each person assessed between two or three team-roles. The points were added up by our research team and we had before us a team-role profile for each member of the syndicate as seen by his fellow members.

PERCEIVED PLANTS AND RESOURCE INVESTIGATORS

Since the Plant formula had been cross-validated in a proper behavioural sense, it was worth seeing how those indicated as Plants on the formula were seen by their fellow members. No uniform picture presented itself. Some individuals indicated as Plants by the psychometric tests were viewed in the same way by members, while other Plants were seen in a variety of different ways, some receiving only a low Plant score. Of further interest to us were cases where there was a consensus that some given syndicate member was a Plant when our test scores pointed to the contrary. What could the explanation be? Was there some other type of ideas man abroad that had so far eluded the net of psychometric tests?

The individuals seen as creative who, on the basis of their test scores were not Plants, were grouped together and their test scores examined. The picture that emerged was that of a group of men with a definite set of characteristics in common. Whereas the Plant had tended towards introversion, this group had scores markedly in the direction of extroversion. At first sight this might suggest that Plants could fall into two types, one of introverted and the other of extroverted disposition, so that they would be variants, so to speak, of the same basic model.

Further examination of the test scores and behaviour of the new group suggested that the explanation was not as simple as that. Plants (certainly good Plants) had been found to be clever, even very clever, as measured by their superior scores on the CTA. This group, however, had only average scores. On the PPQ test there were several notable construct similarities and differences between Plants and our new innovative group. Both groups tended to produce a wide range of responses. There, however, the similarities ended. Plants had a larger number than average of negative constructs (reasons for rejecting items) and their constructs were numerous in the Brain and Originality categories. Clearly they were valuing the qualities they possessed themselves. Our new group, by contrast, had low scores in the construct categories of Brain and Originality. Instead they valued Versatility.

The 16PF recorded further differences between the two groups. Tender-mindedness, natural forthrightness and the introverted tendencies characterizing Plants in the 16PF all vanished in the new group. In their place the scales suggesting sociability and enthusiasm became prominent along with scores indicative of low anxiety. In a word those perceived as Plants but not so identified on the formula could be summed up as inquisitive stable extroverts.

Having isolated this group we now began to look more closely at their behaviour. They were, indeed, men for whom new ideas were a focus of interest. Yet rather than standing out as originators they were more inclined to pick up fragments of ideas from others and develop them. They were particularly adept at exploring resources outside the group. Liaison work gave them just the right opportunity to come back with some new proposition which could often transform *company* plans. They explored resources so well that we came to term them Resource Investigators (RIs).

While both RIs and PLs (Plants) were seen by their colleagues as creative and liable to be confused with each other, extreme examples of the type were distinct. When the PL was held to have a very original mind he was regarded as an oddball and a loner. On the other hand an RI assessed as very creative usually stood out for his close involvement with people and skill in using resources. The more he fulfilled his team-role the more he looked like a manager, whereas the more the PL fulfilled his team-role the less he looked like a manager. The RI was more easily integrated into the management team because his approach to innovation better fitted prevailing managerial axioms.

INNOVATORS IN THE TEAM

It was now plain that a team could benefit from possessing both types of innovator. Their roles were complementary. The PL would sit in a corner on his own, thinking things through and sometimes coming up with some winning possibility; the RI would ensure that no stone was left unturned and would use his special skills to find treasure in unexpected spots. A gifted Chairman would value and use both to advantage.

The contrasting abilities, qualities and style of operation of the PL and RI usually mean that they typically belong to different people but this is not always so. Occasionally the wayward genius of the PL and the resourcefulness of the RI in making the most of interpersonal opportunities are combined in one individual.

A good example we encountered of a PL/RI combination was a participant who attended our three-day team integration seminar. He was by occupation the Advertising Manager of a multinational, later to leave that position to take up an appointment on the staff of the Prime Minister.

At the start of the Teamopoly exercise this clever and highly innovative participant secured for himself the job of attending auctions which was one of three ways of securing property, the others, as previously stated, being by tender and negotiation. Teamopoly was set up – or was meant to be set up – in such a way that no single aspect of a team's activities can dominate the others so as to have an undue bearing on the outcome. At the same time each component of activity needs to fit into or find an appropriate place in a *company's* corporate strategy, even if that strategy is not expressed in any precise plan. In this particular instance, however, the *company* was dominated by the

manoeuvrings of this PL/RI member whose *company* took the lead at
the outset of the exercise and widened it as time went on.

Success in this instance was gained by brilliant play at auction. Our
PL/RI friend attended every auction from start to finish. Whether or not
his *company* was interested in buying any particular piece of property,
he bid for everything that came up. His *company* was presumed by
others to be flush with money secured by some means that were none
too clear. The essence of bidding is to know where to stop and read the
field. Our friend furnished himself with as much information as he
could gather about the finances of other *companies* and their property
holdings. Then he would bid their representatives up as far as he
thought he could go without incurring the risk of being landed with a
property he did not want. At the same time he was constantly on the
lookout for bargains which were most likely to be found right at the
beginning or right at the end of auctions. In due course these cheap
properties became bargaining counters or blocking factors hindering
the easy development of property strategies by rival *companies*.
Whenever the auction arrived at a property that he saw as desirable in
his own strategic plans he was prepared to bid high but with an air of
bored indifference.

The fact that our friend was acting as an inspired independent
operator did not endear him to his *company*. *Company* plans and
decisions were largely ignored. Instead he acted with bravado doing
whatever he thought was most fitting. Only the runaway success
achieved by his adroit performance redeemed him in the eyes of his
company, or part of it. The other part could still not completely forgive
him!

In the above instance the strategic ability of a Plant was combined with
the typical innovative opportunism and presence of mind of the
Resource Investigator. Usually, high-powered strategic thought and the
quickness of mind of someone who thinks on his feet belong to different
people. Then there is the very real danger of acting out of role with
consequences that are less fortunate.

In another seminar we replaced a participant who had had to drop out
at the last minute with a Cambridge scholar who had recently secured
a starred first in his examinations. His test records showed very high
critical thinking and a high Plant score. We placed him in a well-
balanced *company*, short only in brainpower, where his fellow
company members were managers twice his age. The mix initially
seemed a great success. Our Cambridge scholar read the rules and was
soon explaining the complications and niceties to the others. Better
still, he was devising strategies that seemed to him worthwhile and no
less so to his fellow *company* members. The strategies began to pay off
very early and his personal prestige rose immensely in his *company*. A
point was now reached in the game where the focus of attention fell on
the auction. Our rising star felt the urge to diversify his skills and

requested permission to represent *company* interests there. The experienced managers in his *company* recognizing a promising young man, decided to give him his head. Once in the auction area our prodigy appeared a good deal less promising. One or two wily businessmen soon noticed that he was overanxious to secure certain items of property and decided to play him along. Overspending to a degree he had not bargained for, he now found that he could not complete his prior plan. But equally he could not adapt his strategy. He failed to take advantage of one or two adventitious factors which others seized on. A solitary figure amongst the jostling bidders, he returned with an astonishingly poor set of purchases for the money he had taken with him. Nor had he succeeded in negotiating any business with other disappointed bidders holding complementary interests. The *company* which at one stage was leading the field fell back to a position from which it could not recover and finished last.

PLANTS IN THE BUSINESS WORLD

The basic lessons that we learned about the role of Plants in teams, about their triumphs and the mistakes to which they were susceptible, soon took flesh and bones, as it were, as we found ourselves becoming involved one way or another with the real business world. Ironically, while many participants in management courses and seminars were striving to appear as Plants, the realities of life in the outside world showed that Plants were faring none too well. Their very skills and abilities tended to shunt them into specialist technical positions from which they could not escape. Their ambitions to enter into the mainstream of management were usually frustrated by the incarcerating effect which any continued experience has on career development. Less able colleagues would be moved more readily, because they could be spared, and so in time built up a track record which qualified them for senior posts. Most firms have not come to grips with, or are hardly even aware of, this danger.

Long-established organizations seldom have Plants at their heads unless it is in response to a challenge that has disrupted the emphasis on continuity. Then the need for survival demands appointments which in normal circumstances would have been unthinkable.

A firm in the Midlands engaged in the fabrication of plastics for various domestic and industrial purposes had run into financial troubles from which it had difficulty in escaping in spite of the continuous ministerings of its holding company. As is common in such cases the holding company eventually freed itself from its burden by selling the company. An American combine took it over and appointed a

Managing Director with an impeccable business school background. Many changes in systems and controls were introduced but in spite of all efforts no real financial improvement was registered. Another Managing Director succeeded in the temporal but not in the financial sense. The company was sold again. After one further change at the top, an unexpected internal appointment was made: the Technical Director who had been there throughout these changes was made the head of the firm.

The new MD had never taken our test battery so that the depiction of him as a Plant is conjectural. Nevertheless he was undoubtedly a man with a keen analytical mind and something of an introvert, quite lacking in the general exuberance commonly associated with bosses. At the same time he had the forthright boldness that typifies Plants combined with a tendency towards radical thought.

Shortly after he took over, he summoned the Financial Director and they entered into prolonged scrutiny of company finances, discussing all aspects of the premises on which they calculated profitability or unprofitability of the various company products. At that time overheads were proportional to the material and direct labour charges on each product line. One of the company's main selling lines was hand cream tubes which were decorated to the very high specification demanded by the cosmetic market. The production line was virtually automated, the capital cost of the machinery was high and the line itself generated a considerable demand on the services of the skilled engineers. This particular product line was supposed to yield a good profit, but the new MD spotted that as there was little direct labour and only a small amount of plastic was used for each item, there was the chance that overheads were being undercharged. "Why don't we try charging overheads according to the floor space our products take up," he suggested. This new costing exercise was put into operation and soon revealed a markedly different picture of the profitability or otherwise of various product lines. The next step was to consider what would happen if the company were to change its selling prices so as to reflect the costs calculated by the new method. Sales reacted strongly against the prospect but close questioning revealed that what was presumed to be a highly competitive market in large part reflected the keenness and bargaining sense of buyers rather than real market pressures. The defects in the company's costing system were then discussed with a number of leading customers and the new pricing structure was introduced. Within six month's of the MD's appointment the company made a monthly profit for the first time for five years and thereafter never looked back.

While Plant managers are relatively uncommon in secure and established firms and organizations, they are much in evidence in newly formed companies. Abilities and qualities needed to start a firm are very different from those that enable a firm to consolidate its success. A brilliant entrepreneur may therefore become both the reason for a firm's rise and the cause of its downfall. From rags to riches to rags traditionally spans three generations but the progression can take place in one.

Since the war, a university city renowned for its scientific traditions has witnessed the creation of a number of new enterprises associated with advanced technology and the growth of these enterprises has bestowed on the area one of the lowest unemployment rates in the country.

Two Plants in their separate and combined ways have personally exercised a major influence on this growth. Both are Plants in the literal sense in that their test scores follow the classic Plant pattern. One of the Plants in fact qualifies to be called a Superplant.

Plant No. 1 (henceforth known as Mr. Plant) began by carrying out bits of research and development that could be sold to meet the needs of developing companies that lacked technical expertise. A few associates joined in, attracted by the opportunities for self-expression, and a back-of-the-house enterprise was soon operating. It was a firm which carried very few overheads and had no administrators. Any money that was made at the end of the day was shared by those engaged in the work. Recruitment was never a problem. As creative scientists heard about the work and the attractive, co-operative, informal life style, they simply presented themselves at Mr. Plant's door and they were soon down to work. Overcrowding demanded new premises, but with a successful track record and a healthy order book money was found without difficulty.

Meanwhile, Plant No. 2 (henceforth known as Mr. Superplant) had also started in business in much the same way, making electronic kits and selling them through the mail order business. Later, manufacture was put out to subcontractors. This proved a fine stroke as it enabled Mr. Superplant to concentrate his brilliant mind on the design and marketing of new products. The firm grew in a material way, while still remaining a private company. A new advanced product, for which a big market was developing, swept aside the opposition to become the leading seller in Western Europe. Mr. Superplant now had a thriving company in new premises and was being hailed as a business whizz kid. The basic strategy of subcontracting everything he could had enabled Mr. Superplant to use his full gains to advantage, but as his firm grew he became increasingly embroiled in having to manage an enterprise in which a great number of day-to-day decisions had to be made. To some extent he managed to escape from diurnal detail by spreading responsibility amongst executives in his firm but the firm remained largely an extension of himself. He would fly to the U.S. to promote one of his products only to overrule on his return decisions made in his absence.

Success sometimes creates its own problems. The firm of Mr. Plant had now spawned subsidiaries on the backs of its own inventions and technological advances. A serious mistake was now made in setting up a company to manufacture the products it had designed. Highly inventive, but somewhat anarchic, individuals are seldom good at coping with the disciplines and exigencies of modern production; and it was in keeping that they had already filed their objections to filling in time sheets so as to allow development costs to be calculated, seeing them as a bureaucratic infringement of their freedom. As manufacturers they began collectively to fail, sucking down with them their profitable R & D base. A rescue operation was mounted by a takeover company. The tough terms demanded were that a new chief executive should be appointed to head the group, a businessman of proven ability – none other than Mr. Superplant! The rescue proved abortive, the receiver was called in and the bits and pieces were sold off. The hard and still profitable core of the business of which Mr. Plant was the focus was bought by a leading US concern with interests in the same field. Eventually Mr. Plant who had already lost his role as chief executive, was fired. The thriving firm that he had founded finally cast him out!

The would-be rescuer, Mr. Superplant, was meanwhile getting into difficulties himself. His leading product that at one time had swept all before it was rapidly losing its share of the market. It was not simply imitation by the big boys that was undermining it. The product, along with a number of other products which his company marketed, had acquired a poor reputation for reliability. Instead of working to improve the quality of his products and consolidate their success, or passing responsibility for so doing onto someone else, Mr. Superplant escaped by stressing in his advertising the generous terms of his guarantees. In offering to replace without question any product that failed, he conveniently in practice passed on that duty to subcontractors. Undiverted by the pressing needs of established products, he was able to turn his full attention to new developments.

Mr. Superplant was now designing a world-beating new product. Technically it was going well but the development costs were proving high and the steady income once afforded by profitable old products were no longer there. The bank refused all further loans. Faced with the prospect of bankruptcy our Superplant had to accept a takeover bid and the great one-man empire began to crumble. The stage had been reached when a Plant was to give way to an organization man!

That Plants in difficulty cannot be rescued by other Plants would seem to be a simple rule worth observing. At an even more fundamental level is the lesson that Plants, and, even more so, Superplants, have a specifically creative role to play in a management team but that if they act out of role their asset value is greatly reduced.

QUALITIES OF RESOURCE INVESTIGATORS

Let us turn now to our other innovative character, whom we have chosen to know as a Resource Investigator. It is easy to recognize and to understand his style of operation once we witness characteristic examples of his behaviour. The RI is uninhibited about finding out what he wants to know by making good use of other people. It is the way in which he naturally operates. Conversation is skilfully directed towards creative ends.

One striking example of the behaviour of a Resource Investigator (in this case one with high mental ability) was furnished by a participant attending our first team-building seminar in Sydney. The venue was a management training centre situated in an attractive location that was virtually in the bush yet not far from the sea. As it happened, we had decided to introduce an innovation in this seminar following a fortuitous event that had worked out well in the previous seminar in Melbourne. There we had been on the point of holding an auction during the Teamopoly exercise in a corridor, when to our consternation, workmen arrived to fix a wall telephone at the very place we had chosen. Our auctioneer, playing for time, wrote on the blackboard that the venue would be announced shortly. Then, being something of a wit, he wrote down a clue that referred to a room by a name known only to those that worked at the college where the seminar was being held. All the participants ran round the rooms looking for the auctioneer (who was hiding) and only one person had the presence of mind to ask someone who seemed likely to know what the cryptic message meant. The answer gave him an advantage to which all the others later objected. The RI in question, who had been the one to ask, rejoined: "I used resources; why didn't you?"

This time we decided to set up a similar situation intentionally. At a key point in the exercise a merry jingle on the blackboard announced the venue of the auction: "Where the water falls free, there shall auction be."

None of the participants seemed unduly concerned by the indefinite nature of the message. But as the time for the auction drew nigh, there was a general scurrying towards the bathrooms and water closets. At that point our rather bright RI began to feel that there was more to the message than met the eye. He became aware that there was only one person around on the permanent staff of the centre who might be able to furnish the missing link – the telephonist/receptionist.

"Can you tell me if there is any form of free-flowing water round here?", he enquired.

"Yes," she said. "There is a waterfall about 100 yards downstream".

"Good," our friend said. "And tell me, is there no free-flowing water upstream?".

"No," she replied but then on reflection added, "but there is a very small weir upstream."

"Even better," our friend replied. "And lastly," he continued, "can you tell me also if anyone else has asked the same question?"

Finding out the answer was no, our RI then devised the useful ruse of despatching his *company*'s usual buyer at auctions to the upper weir loudly proclaiming his intentions, as he himself made off to the lower waterfall. There he was pleased to find the auctioneer waiting ready. As the stentorian voice of the auctioneer boomed details of London property for sale, a bevy of Australian executives now at the upper weir fought their way through the bush towards the voice. As the hot, torn and tumbling latecomers slithered down the bank to the quiet spot where the auctioneer was standing, they were none too pleased to see a colleague calmly standing there with the deeds of a cheaply bought property already in his hand. At the inquest indignant objections were raised: yet no one could think of a good reason why they should not also have asked the way and reached the same conclusion about the venue of the auction.

Resource Investigators get around, find out what is going on, meet people, and pose well thought-out questions. Mottram's definition of a Resource Investigator is that, "he is the executive who is never in his room and, if he is, he's on the phone". In consequence RIs have the knack of doing business. But they have no less a facility for getting new things started.

The ability to relate and communicate with people seems to be a necessary feature of an RI. One good example of a person whose RI scores were highlighted at one of our team-building seminars was a man who headed an industrial training establishment in the private sector originally confined to a single industry. Under his leadership this establishment, though in competition with public sector training bodies, had expanded its functions to cover management education and training in all industries. Our RI became a regular at the various seminars and training courses which the Industrial Training Research Unit ran at Cambridge and in due course was to become the first licensee of one of the ITRU's best-selling industrial products, thereby stealing a march on a number of similar organizations in the same field. Had our RI been a research man himself, it would have been arguable that a research man with industrial experience knows best how to use research. But no, our RI had a most unlikely background. In his early days he had been a comedian, working the northern halls. At one ITRU conference we had made him Chairman and he had succeeded in bringing tears of laughter to delegates even in such an unpromising role as introducing a speaker. A comedian masters his art by timing. By timing, too, a Resource Investigator knows when to strike, when to ask the right question, and how to spot the occasion back home that will benefit from the fitting introduction of a new idea.

We have seen in this chapter that the sheer production of ideas is no measure of a team's creativity. Rather it seems that creativity is one aspect of a team's functioning but it is an aspect that needs to be covered well. We have identified two types of people within a team: the Plant and the Resource Investigator, who in their different ways possess special skills in furnishing the innovative element that the team requires. Whether a team can take advantage of it or not depends on a number of factors, not least of which is the team's leadership.

5: Team Leadership

The quickest and surest way of changing the fortunes of a firm is to replace the man at the top. This formula for success has become the stock in trade of those who deal with or take over ailing organizations. There is so much experience to support and reinforce this approach that the critical role of leadership in determining corporate performance can be taken for granted. Leadership is always vital and team leadership is no exception.

That being so, what are the characteristics of the man who best leads in a complex problem-solving environment where he is supported by an able set of executives? This seems a straightforward enough question. But a straightforward answer is not possible without first clarifying the question further. Is the best leader the one who is most acceptable to the group, with the personal behaviour and image that most fits what people look for in a leader? Or is the best leader the one most likely, during the tenure of his office, to enable the team to reach its goals? That important differences exist between elected and effective leaders is well attested in the research literature. Unfortunately for the cause of democracy, elected leaders are not necessarily effective in achieving their goals. If a choice is to be made between these two types of leader, then from a management standpoint there is only one option: the effective leader has to be chosen. A more popular but less effective leader creates a fool's paradise with long-term benefits being sacrificed for short-term gain. The very essence of a manager is that he achieves the goals he sets himself or which belong to that corporate body of which he is a part.

EXPERIMENTS WITH CHAIRMEN

Taking a pragmatic view on leadership, we set about examining the records of the first seventy-five *companies* competing in the EME. The method was simply to divide the *companies* into three groups in terms of their financial results (good, intermediate and bad) and to scrutinize the psychometric test data of the person acting as Chairman of each group (each *company* had elected a Chairman). We therefore ended up with three sets of profiles for leader. In terms of the personality measures the profiles of those in the intermediate group fell somewhere between the scores of Chairmen of the good and bad *companies*. In fact there were some sharp differences between the 16PF scores of the successful and unsuccessful Chairmen. From these data a formula was developed which stood up well to further test and analysis in the courses that followed our initial studies. In other words, the outcome for these *companies*, in terms of financial results, depended in no small part on the measured personality attributes of the man in the Chair.

Mental Ability and Creativity

Mental ability was of course also an important variable. Before we begin to consider the differences between successful and unsuccessful Chairmen in this respect, it is as well to reflect on what results might reasonably have been expected. Our measures included high level reasoning ability (the CTA) and we had, in addition, as we have already seen, some discriminating measures of creativity based on personality dimensions. While we might believe that clever and creative Chairmen would be at an advantage we have to bear in mind the possible differences between being a Chairman of a *company* in a management game and being a management leader in a firm or institution. In the latter position long-standing experience and political skill might compensate for any limitations in intellectual or problem-solving ability. This is not to deny the value of high mental ability as a generally useful asset in management: the point rather is to emphasize that if analytical ability, judgement, and creativity are important in Chairmen or management team leaders in highly stable situations in which knowledge and experience grow steadily, then these same assets must have importance *a fortiori* in a complicated and unfamiliar management game. Turning these assumptions into a definite set of expectations we could hypothesize that in the management game the *companies* with the most successful financial results would have Chairmen with high scores in mental ability and creativity; conversely, the Chairmen whose *companies* produced the worst results were likely to be relatively low in mental ability and creativity.

That hypothesis seemed to reflect no more than simple common sense. Indeed every argument seemed to point in its favour. But the facts argued otherwise. Successful Chairmen were not *on average* more mentally able nor more creative than their less successful counterparts. The management game was clearly not distorting reality by over-emphasizing high mental ability.

Once our most promising hypothesis was out of the way, we could begin to look at what did constitute the ingredients for success. The successful Chairman was at least up to the (measured) mental ability of his colleagues yet not very far ahead of them. The average Critical Thinking Appraisal score of all the Henley executives (including overseas members, graduates and non-graduates) was 74. The best range in CTA score for the successful Henley Chairman lay between 75 and 80. Slightly less successful were Chairmen with scores above 80 but not exceeding 85. Much less successful were the two extreme groups. A major bearing on the success rate of the Chairman was a set of personality factors derived from the personality inventory (see below). These factors could be compounded into a formula, known as the "successful Chairman formula". One of the points noted was that the predictive power of this formula was modified in a less than simple fashion by the mental ability index where either the formula or the index lay outside an ideal range. It worked in this way. Chairmen with low scores in measured mental ability tended to be associated with poor *company* results but these results were better than expected if they obtained good scores on the successful Chairman formula. Chairmen with very high scores in the CTA also did poorly, with few exceptions, but were less subject to the favourable influences of the formula. In other words it seemed that Chairmen with less than desirable mental ability for the job could compensate to some extent through character attributes. On the other hand high mental ability in a Chairman tended to overshadow the effects of personality.

Personality Attributes

Since the personality inventory proved a useful indicator of the successful team leader it is revealing to sum up what was learned about his typical characteristics. He was in the first place trusting by nature, accepting people as they were without jealousy or suspicion. Counterbalancing this acceptance was a strong basic dominance to which was added an equally strong and morally based commitment to external goals and objectives. Finally, a third, larger set of miscellaneous factors was added: the successful Chairman was calm and unflappable in the face of controversy; he was geared towards practical realism; he possessed a basic self-discipline; he was naturally enthusiastic with that extrovert capacity for excitement that is known to motivate others yet he was no pure extrovert for he was prone to detachment and distance in social relations. One additional point of interest concerned the scores as a measure of group orientation. Those with high scores were seldom appointed or elected Chairmen! It was as if the group selected as their leader one member who was not, as it were, a typical product of the group. Hartston, who was responsible for the analysis of Chairman scores, has summed up these data with a new definition of the successful Chairman. "Someone tolerant enough always to listen to others but strong enough to reject their advice."

In due course we were able to add to the profile of a successful Chairman by examining his construct scores on the PPQ. The successful Chairman emerged as a man who thought in very positive terms (the absence of negative words being a feature of his scores on this test); he used constructs which showed approval in particular for people who accomplished their goals and who engaged in struggle and effort; while he clearly liked people who were lively and dynamic. In all these respects, his scores were higher than those of his fellow team members.

Our total set of "good Chairman" predictors played a major part in contributing to our *company* forecasts in the EME. If the person who took up the role of Chairman obtained a high score on our Chairman profile, we marked up the likelihood that his *company* would obtain a good result. Conversely, if the Chairman had a poor score on our formula we marked down the *company's* chances of success.

The "good Chairman" profile was in no way affected by what we might earlier have been led to expect. It was totally the product of what the facts revealed in the search for a formula which best differentiated between those who were most effective in getting results and those who were least effective.

IMPLICATIONS OF RESULTS

At this point a certain amount of rationalization would not come amiss. Why, we may ask ourselves, should such a man prove so successful, when his personal qualities and abilities are hardly in line with those that scrutiny of the game would suggest as a desirable specification for winning it?

To answer this question we have to consider the implications of the scores that did mark out our successful Chairman. These suggest that the man at the helm was not the man who was personally showing his flock the way through the maze of difficult problems that beset a *company* in this complex exercise. In the last chapter we identified just the man with the creative flair who might have done this. We called him the Plant. Evidently a Plant acting as Chairman would have conferred less advantage on his company than the sort of man that our pragmatic study has revealed. What then are the real assets of this team leader? In a word the ideal Chairman looks like a manager – a man who knows how to use resources, who is singularly adaptive when it comes to people but who never loses his grip on a situation or his ability to reach his own judgement based on his assessment of what is needed in practice.

While this ideal Chairman specification seems also to fit that of a manager, the two should not be seen as coinciding. Not all managers are ideal leaders of teams. Some managers barely conceal their impatience with teams, with committees or indeed with anything that smacks of group leadership. Other managers possess such singular talents that their staff are essentially supportive: they make the decisions and give their staff explicit directives so that quite senior men still act, often intuitively, as though under day-to-day instruction even when the boss is out of the country.

The Chairman-manager seems very different. That he has a distinctive style of managing was apparent from the reports which the observers in the exercise were able to furnish. The successful Chairman was not all that dissimilar from other team members but he did stand out as one who carried the respect of others. His interventions were most apparent at critical points in the exercise. Then he would be the man in command, striving to pull the whole thing together. He would never allow meetings to get out of hand. At moments of dissension, he was ever ready to impart a sense of direction and purpose.

Why should the effective Chairman, so distinguished in some ways, tend to have only average scores in mental ability?

Here case studies provided useful leads, especially in relation to Chairmen whose mental ability varied appreciably from the average of the group being either less clever than colleagues or a good deal more clever. Curiously enough extremes produced in their different ways a common difficulty. Both were associated with a loss in a facility for communicating easily with fellow team members.

Mental Ability, Communication, and Control

Take the less clever Chairman. Two typical reactions were observed.

Unable to follow all the various ins and outs of the argument or the intricacy of some of the proposals that were being advanced, he was commonly inclined to opt out of proceedings, failing to exert his authority or pull his group together when it faced conflicting opinions. What was seen as "some lack of contact with members" or even "lack of control" had its roots in a failure to comprehend the nature of the alternatives that were being put forward or to understand the arguments behind them. This Chairman often gave the impression of indecisiveness, being reluctant to make any personal stand. The group tended to lose direction and so became marked by unresolved dissension.

The other observed pattern was virtually the opposite. The Chairman hung on to control and conducted matters in a firm but oversimple fashion. Decisions would be taken without adequately exploring the options or following up either the tentative objections of dissenters or their counter-proposals. The Chairman looked for a majority view and he was over-ready to turn that view into a decision at the first opportunity.

Now let us consider the clever Chairman. He would seem on the face of it to have every advantage over one short in mental ability. Yet clever Chairmen performed no better, although their results were more variable; that is to say in a few cases results were good, in other cases indifferent, while a poor result tended to be the more common outcome. The clever Chairman seemed prone to get the worst of both worlds. His inclination to exercise his skills of control, organization, and attention to detail tended to be undermined by the distracting lure of difficult problems. Either way he never quite fulfilled himself. His sharp mind enabled him to keep ahead of the others but in so doing he was liable to lose touch. While being quick to see any flaws in suggestions put forward by others his own ideas were liable to be based on lines of argument that his team members did not always follow. In some cases his dominance was so complete that the team became in effect a vehicle for his own highly personalized strategy. In such instances communication could break down completely. The Chairman's intellectual authority together with the status which his position conferred on him became enough in some instances to discourage any prospective opponents or even advocates of caution. Members failed to report facts or figures that fell within their own orbits of responsibility that might have caused inconvenience or difficulties for "the plan". The Chairman would end up on his own and not too many tears were shed by other members of the group when the plan misfired!

The Chairman with good average mental ability seemed better placed.

Intellectually he was on much the same wavelength as the others: if they couldn't understand something, neither could he; what they could follow, he could too. Communication operated freely in both directions. Hence when one team member possessed evident capacities for criticism or suggestions of a superior kind, he was usually quick to see such talent in the team as a bonus of which use had to be made. There was no reason to feel exposed by the demonstration that one member of his team was ahead of the rest of the field (including himself). His decisiveness showed in knowing whom to back.

The ideal Chairman seemed, in terms of the data we had about him, to possess a set of perfectly commonplace characteristics, yet characteristics which were put together in an uncommon way. So unusual was the combination, that we had, in fact, considerable difficulty in finding individuals who displayed all the combinations of attributes that our empirical study of the effective Chairman had revealed. When our ideal Chairman did emerge he still looked an ordinary team member in some respects yet his results could be outstanding.

Perhaps the word *he* is a little unfair. A good example of one ideal Chairman (on our formula) was a woman. Edna Mainstay was a practical, sensible lady of character with no pretensions to intellectual distinction, holding a very senior appointment in her profession. When we composed the team of which she was a member we included a brilliant but difficult person along with a lively communicator who looked as though he would get around well outside the group and ensure that the group would not lose touch with its environment. An observer recorded with copious notes all that happened. Edna was made Chairman and the *company* ended up with a final result well ahead of its other seven rivals in the field. Throughout the exercise the right people seemed to do the right thing at the right time. The observer gave no credit to the Chairman for her control over the proceedings, merely noting that she did not take a leading role. The two leading members of the group took a different view, praising her rather than each other or themselves. Skill in consultation, delegation of work and firmness of decisions all earned high marks. Edna eventually joined one of our early seminars on management team-building and so took part in Teamopoly. As the teams consisted of only four members, the role of Chairman is often left vacant and the members operate instead as a closely knit group. In this instance, however, she was made Chairman in a formal sense. Again she was inconspicuous in the way in which she performed her duties but each team member found himself naturally cast in the right job. Everything fell into place and the team won. "In my professional role I am used to working with consultants on committees," our Chairman declared, "and I think I know how to get the best out of them."

It is quite difficult to identify individuals with this gift for it belongs to some deceptively ordinary people. The ability to act well in the Chair is in itself not an uncommon accomplishment. But the value of this skill falls a good deal short of the ability to obtain a first rate result from a team over which a Chairman presides.

OTHER LEADERSHIP QUALITIES

The Management Team-building seminars that we set up after our experience with experimental companies at Henley attracted a new range of people including some in very senior positions. Group Personnel Managers for multinational organizations were well represented and there was a fair number of successful Managing Directors who were now interested in finding executive teams to spawn subsidiary companies. Amongst this senior group we expected to find a good proportion of men with the typical Chairman profile. We were surprised to find that this was not so. We had developed a leadership formula through painstaking research which we had put to the test by giving it a key position in our forecasting formulae. These forecasts had stood up to the test well, admittedly not in all cases, but to an extent that gave grounds for belief that we were well and truly on the right track. Now we were faced with the surprising phenomenon that a substantial class of known leaders did not accord with the general shape of the profile. They did not even resemble them. What then was the explanation?

The immediate thought was that some differences existed between artificial team games of the sort that are practised in management training establishments and the reality of team leadership in the business and institutional world. If this were so, we could have been acting on the wrong specification, recommending to industry men who might make good captains for teams in artificial games but who might fall down on the job in leading real teams. This seemed an obvious danger. What was needed was evidence either to confirm or dismiss this possibility.

The first question was whether our effective Chairmen performed well as team leaders in the organizations from which they came. The evidence that came our way was necessarily personalized and informal. We were looking especially for qualitative information: did they have any characteristic management style? Where did their personal strengths lie? We did not get hold of all the information that we would have liked but the Henley grapevine and system of personal contacts can work remarkably well when the need arises. The message that came back seemed unequivocal enough. The abilities that these individuals

possessed in their jobs seemed to lie very much in the qualities of
leadership which we had already attributed to them in the training
exercise.

A second question concerned the experience gained with the good
Chairman profile in making placements in industry or in making
adjustments in team balance. Had these worked out in practice or not?

By now we had carried out a good deal of work in industry in using the
strategies, and techniques that we had developed in management team-
building and the Chairmanship profile had stood up well. In the field of
computer applications several field experiences had proved rewarding.
Leaders of project teams had been appointed on the basis of
"Chairmanship" scores rather than on the basis of experience and
seniority, and favourable outcomes had been reported.

> Another notable experience had been with a product development
> team in plastics. This team had not met with much commercial
> success. By chance the Project Leader was transferred to another job.
> A new man moved in whose personal knowledge of the technology
> was rather scant and whose Chairmanship profile did not make him an
> obvious choice to "chair" the project. As it happened the No. 2 in the
> team had an impressive Chairmanship score. The new manager seized
> on the opportunity and said "Why don't you take the Chair? I would far
> prefer to act as the backbench MP and direct myself to criticisms of the
> front bench." This somewhat unorthodox procedure was set in
> motion. The whole experiment worked well. The re-formed project
> team soon made a major impact in its chosen business field and the
> effectiveness of its management teamwork was hailed as the
> cornerstone of its achievement.

None of this evidence suggested that our team leader profile was
missing the mark. So we had to search for other explanations of why so
many senior managers were different from the team leaders highlighted
by our experiments.

Non-Chairman Leaders

The explanation which now seemed likely was that a good proportion of
the proven managers at our seminars belonged to a distinctive group of
effective leaders, who tended to thrive in and to be thrown up by
particular types of environment. If this was so, there was the prospect of
a cluster of managerial characteristics that had not previously come to
light in our studies and of which we had now necessarily to take account.
The problem was that in the personal counselling session which we
afforded each seminar participant we always had something to say
about how a given individual's strengths and abilities might be used to

advantage in contributing to the collective effort of the team. For these people we had little to offer that was constructive. We could not equate these successful leaders with any of the team types (see also Chapter Six) found essential or desirable for the success of a team. For the moment their role and contribution was an uncertain one.

The general impression of the proven top men to which the evidence both of their test profiles and behaviour in the exercise contributed was that of extroverts abounding in nervous energy and actuated by the need for achievement. In many ways they were the antithesis of team men. They challenged; argued; disagreed. They were impatient and easily frustrated. Their proneness to aggression would produce a reciprocal reaction from other team members yet they would respond with remarkably good humour and resilience as though they thoroughly enjoyed a battle. Winning was the name of the game as far as they were concerned and learning was very much the secondary objective. If their team was doing poorly they would question the rules or the fairness of the umpiring, yet they had no hesitation in pursuing their goals by illicit means including on one occasion arson in Cambridge (setting fire to a rival *company's* paperwork plans when they were temporarily out of the room!). Once the game had ended and concentration on winning could be set aside, a new and sudden interest erupted in the lessons for the future, in the way in which the message could be put across back at the firm. The more poorly the members' *companies* had performed, the greater the intensity of their interest, in spite of their smarting at the mistakes which they, or more usually in their eyes another member of the team, had made.

We christened this recognizable group of executives Shapers. We now had two types of team leader, abbreviated to CH and SH. In due course we formed companies of Shapers in our Teamopoly exercises for the purpose of learning something more about them. They never failed to illustrate for our seminar participants how the character of a *company* can be moulded by the team-types that are enrolled. Whether they did well or poorly they always created uproar. In a seminar we ran in Canberra for government officials one *company* of Shapers spent a good deal of time successfully disrupting other rival *companies* both by legitimate and illegitimate means. While the behaviour by government officials surprised us at the time it was mild by comparison with our last experience in Melbourne. There a team of Shapers, that had sunk into a bad last place through extravagant overbidding and a failure to co-ordinate their plans effectively, resorted to desperate antics. These included securing a live pistol with a view to kidnapping the auctioneer (failing as it happened through a change of venue), stealing money from the bank followed by a demand for money for "information received", and holding a lady member of the winning team hostage by brute force for the purpose of ransom. This tomfoolery helped dispel the tension caused by not winning and provided an alternative and enjoyable form of substitute achievement. With infamous conduct being a not uncommon feature of such *companies* my colleague, Neil Stucley, was stimulated to enrich the English – or at least the Australian – language. He invented a new collective noun: a shockery of Shapers.

Research had started into the qualities and attributes of Shapers soon after their basic symptoms were observed and recorded. The Shaper became the eighth specification drawn up and used by Henley members for the purpose of establishing each individual's best team-role, in the eyes of his fellow syndicate members. Earlier we had used the team-role perception inventory in the study of creative members (pp. 153-7) and now we found it had application to the study of team leaders. The method, as before, was to allocate ten points to be distributed between the team-roles to which the member was judged as being fitted in the view of the assessor. All ten points could be given, and sometimes were, to a single team-role, in which case the affinity for that team-role was judged as being very strong indeed; or they could be spread more widely. The scores from all the assessors were then combined and added together for each person assessed and from this a person's best team-role could be judged. Each individual judged also made his own self-assessment allocating the ten points just as if he were judging another. By using this technique in two successive courses we ended up with over one hundred assessments and self-assessments and from these we could pick the individual whose assessments and self-assessments were in close agreement as indicative of Shaper.

After our sample of SHs had been obtained in this way we worked back to their test scores so that for forecasting purposes we could establish what type of test profile made a Shaper. Statistically the data gave the highest loadings on apprehension, suspicion, proneness to frustration, and sociability. Additionally the Shaper was opportunistic rather than conscientious, tough-minded, emotional, but free from shyness and social timidity. All this suggested a tough anxious extrovert, a man prone to overreact to disappointments or annoyances but resilient, fearless, and unflinching with people.

Shapers in Teams

As we gained experience in introducing Shapers individually into teams and in composing teams consisting entirely of Shapers, we began to appreciate that Shapers had very definite pros and cons. There was never any doubt that a Shaper-led group would be galvanized into action. If a group was prone to complacency or inaction, the presence of a Shaper restored the balance so that performance improved. On the other hand a Shaper was usually a disruptive force in a well-balanced group, especially one led by someone with typical Chairman profile. A Shaper could spoil a well-established team. Collectively, Shapers did not have too bad a record as far as results were concerned. A team of Shapers tended to generate its own culture, often achieving a high work rate, being quick to explore all possible avenues of approach and abandoning any that did not look rewarding. However, they seldom liked working with each other and could see that a team built on their lines would sooner or later run into difficulties. In spite of a great deal of positive goal-directed activity, the damaging consequences of in-fighting tended to lead to poor results. In these cases the combination of aggravation and failure was too much to bear. People were only too ready to testify to the sins of the culprit most responsible and to give full vent to their indignation.

CHAIRMEN AND SHAPERS AS LEADERS

The effective Chairman profile and the Shaper profile gave us two approaches to leadership. The most reliable results, both in our own training exercises and in the industrial assignments on which we worked, were yielded by the effective Chairman profile. Yet known leaders outside Henley were more likely to display the Shaper profile. How could we explain this seeming paradox?

There seemed two likely levels of explanation. One was that the highly active, dynamic, restless manager may be less attracted to a ten-week interlude in management education in a quiet beauty spot of the Chilterns than in presenting himself for a three-day seminar where there was the prospect that he might pick up something useful quickly. Certainly we detected over the years a population difference, with a good supply of Chairmen and a scarcity of Shapers at Henley against an abundance of Shapers and a dearth of Chairmen in our seminars.

Another part of the explanation must relate to a basic bifurcation to which the whole field of leadership is subject. There is a strong situational difference between leading a group in a directive way and marshalling the resources of a team, especially where that team is well equipped to tackle a complex set of interrelating problems. Many organizations present some sort of dilemma where the leadership is concerned and the question of complexity lies at the very heart of the matter. As well as complexity of problems there is another type – political complexity. Where issues require concerted action by people operating at different levels and subject to their own, sometimes conflicting, set of rules, regulations, and constraints, inertia almost inevitably sets in. In dealing with the stagnation which this political complexity generates, the Shaper thrives. He is effective in gingering up slow-moving systems or even in changing the way in which they function so that certain ends may be achieved. Provided he is right in his analysis, the Shaper makes such a positive impact that he is bound to be promoted.

In our Teamopoly exercises Shapers seemed to do well individually when the role of Chairman was bestowed upon them. Our seminar exercise seemed more suited to their leadership talents than did the EME. In the former there were various ways in which action and initiative were rewarded. Effective planning and co-ordination still played a part but had a less all-embracing influence than in the EME. We had designed Teamopoly so as to incorporate, as we saw it, the main body of skills that are crucial in top management. Success can be gained by more than one route. One avenue was open for the sort of skills that Shapers possess. By being themselves and using their natural drive, persistence and high pressure negotiating skills to advantage, they were capable of outmanoeuvring the other *companies*. But where this outmanoeuvring failed, they had less to fall back on than the classic Chairman.

Just as there are horses for courses, so there are leaders for teams. We have established, perhaps, or attempted to establish two archetypal leaders, one combining skilful use of the reserves of the group with the effective control of team members (the CH type) and the other an instigator of action (the SH type), who as often as not succeeds by dragging the team along with him. Clearly the nature of the challenge and the characteristics of the team members both have a bearing on which of these two leaders best suits a situation.

APOLLO CHAIRMEN

While CH and SH team leaders between them can cover most situations, there was one more team leader that our studies finally managed to reveal. This was the leader best fitted to cope with a team comprising individuals of very high mental ability, typically an Apollo team as we christened it in Chapter Two. This team was susceptible to under-achievement: their corporate capability fell short of the standards expected by reason of the individual abilities of those who formed the team. While such teams tended to perform poorly even in comparison with run-of-the-mill *companies*, there were some instances where Apollo teams encountered the usual difficulties but overcame them to finish strongly. In these instances the Chairman appeared to play an important part. We therefore became interested in successful Apollo Chairmen. Were they closer to the CH or the SH type of leader?

In one respect successful Apollo Chairmen were like other successful Chairmen by being slightly, and only slightly, cleverer than the groups over which they were presiding. In practice of course this made them cleverer than the general run of successful Chairmen since Apollos were cleverer than other groups. In other respects Apollo Chairmen were unlike our classic Chairmen, showing a number of Shaper traits. Yet they were not really Shapers for they lacked the Shaper's restless desire to lead from the front. The main distinguishing feature of the Apollo Chairmen, as revealed by analysis of their psychometric test scores, was a marked rise in those personality scores suggesting suspicion and scepticism compensated by a small fall in dominance and a move away from the concern for practical matters towards an interest in broad essentials.

These results made sense to us, especially when they were supplemented by observer reports which indicated the successful Apollo Chairman's style of operation. The essential behavioural difference between the classic CH and the Apollo CH leader lies in the approach to the group. The classic CH leader is adept at drawing out the potential of the group; he recognizes and encourages all those aspects of talent and ability that must be cultivated if the team is to achieve its objectives; he is past master, for example, at spotting and developing the creative flair of the individual who would normally lie submerged in the group of which he is a member. The Apollo CH leader on the other hand is less of a searcher after talent; rather he is a tough discriminating person who can hold his ground in any company; yet he never dominates.

CONCLUSION

To sum up then, we can claim to have detected, and with the aid of our psychometric test instruments we think we can select, three distinctive types of team leader. One is suited for the balanced team that, due to its team-role distribution, possesses at a number of levels the potential for coping with complex multidimensional problems; another fits the team that has the established capability to do well but which faces obstacles that are either internal or external; and the third type is appropriate to the "think tank" type of team. The classic CH, the SH and the Apollo

CH are the leaders that correspond with and are appropriate to these teams between which we find it useful to distinguish.

What can be said about team leaders who cannot be equated with any one of our three types and whose personal qualities and characteristics are altogether different? Some have long established and proven competence as team leaders or as formal Chairmen of committees. In these cases effectiveness in running teams has usually been learned in a gradual way. A person who has proved his worth in some part of the managerial orbit often endeavours to become effective in other fields towards which he possesses no natural aptitude. The very challenge motivates him to respond. A manager gifted with high intelligence and a capacity for balanced judgement may be so shy and self-effacing (on the evidence of test data) that it is difficult to conceive of him discharging some of the responsibilities associated with high office. Yet he rises to the occasion. He acts exactly in the way required. His performance is atypical of his normal, natural behaviour. Provided not too many calls are made upon him to act in this way he survives and may even at times distinguish himself. But if he becomes overloaded with demands that pressurize him away from his natural and preferred role he begins not infrequently to look around for another job or chooses early retirement.

Whether an individual manager who is not typically a team leader possesses the talent and readiness to lead a team depends on whether he can develop over time a convincing style of leadership that suits his personality. But it must also depend on the extent of the fit between himself and the team. How far does he supply something that the team lacks? Here we have to learn more about what a good team needs and about the range of contributions from the team members that keep it in balance.

6: Key Team-Roles

By now, we have established some of the primary characters for successful teams. It may be useful to sum up what we already know; why and how these chosen characters make their mark; and what is missing if we are to present the full complement of characters from which all the requirements of the various team models can be met.

COMPANY WORKER

Our starting point had been the identification, through the complex process of statistical inference, of the person we chose to call in Chapter Three the Company Worker. *Companies* in the management game with a higher proportion of such people in their teams tended to get better results. We were also to learn later that Company Workers figured prominently in positions of responsibility in larger organizations.

The term Company Worker does not sound very glamorous. Disappointment was sometimes expressed by managers who found themselves typified as Company Workers either as a result of the tests they took or as a consequence of the peer group rating exercise we had developed. Colleagues and experienced practitioners in the science of team-building sometimes tried the alternative titles of Implementer or Organizer, either of which had the advantage of being marginally better received but the disadvantage of less aptly expressing the real nature of the contribution which this particular member made to the corporate effort. The Company Worker was not simply a man who did or arranged things (most work involves both). In behavioural terms he was a person who essentially worked *for the company*, rather than in pursuit of self-interest, and did so in a practical and realistic way. He could identify with the organization. He would accept and look for goals in work which became, as it were, part of the moral order. There was never any question that a job would not be done because he did not feel like it or it did not interest him. His capacity for disciplined application was a function of his attitude and character against which natural aptitude or intelligence seemed almost of secondary importance. Being disciplined himself he would tend to have an orderly approach to the work before him. Any flair that he might possess nearly always lay in organizational ability.

In large, well-structured organizations such people become very promotable. It is an irony that, while the image of the Company Worker tended to have only a limited appeal to managers, the ranks of Managing Directors, we were to find, contained as many people with Company Worker affinities as with any other role. It has been claimed that the Company Worker characteristic is a common commodity and in consequence surprise is expressed that Company Worker qualities can be associated with the highest ranks of office. Here we would argue that ideal Company Worker qualities are much rarer than people realize. One definition of a Managing Director is that he is the manager who tackles the jobs that nobody else will do. There is a strong grain of truth in this. Many people in practice only do the sort of jobs that appeal to them and neglect those which they find distasteful. There is no great joy, for example, in disciplining a negligent employee or removing from a job someone whose work has not reached the necessary standard. The Company Worker scores over a period of time because he systematically sets about doing the sort of jobs that need to be done in management even though they may be far from intrinsically interesting or pleasant. This is a great test of character strength, quite at variance with what is implied by the notion of the "organization man". The pejorative attached to this straw figure has gained impetus from the influence of Whyte's famous book *The Organization Man*, and reflects the anti-industrial value systems so prevalent in large sections of the academic world. The Company Man has been portrayed as an individual bereft of individual personality, fashioned by the moulding hand of the all pervasive company, so that he lives his life as a diminished figure only capable of certain acts that are prescribed for him. If this evident weakling exists in positions of responsibility, he has little in common with the Company Worker who has emerged from our intensive studies. Both men face the constraints of the system of which they are a necessary part. The difference seems to be that in the one case the individual succumbs to the pressures which the system places upon him, while in the other the individual not only meets its needs but in the process grows in stature.

TEAM-ROLE IN PAIRS

To the Company Worker as an essential member of a team we have already seen the case for adding two sets of paired roles. In Chapter Five we examined two types of team leader: our most reliably successful Chairman (CH), adept at drawing on the resources of the group to advantage; and our driving, action-based leader, the Shaper (SH). In Chapter Four we looked at another pair of related roles which govern the creativity of the team; the essentially introverted, very clever, Plant (PL), the subject of so many of our experiments; and the more outgoing, extroverted, inquisitive Resource Investigator (RI).

The existence and evident value of these pairs remind us, on a philosophical note, of how balances are achieved in nature. In physics every particle or force has a corresponding antiparticle or antiforce and all stable systems in the universe depend, so it is held, on the interconnections of constituent opposites.

With this in mind it may be fruitful to reconsider our two pairs of team-roles before proceeding to ask whether anything is missing if the pattern of our rounded team is to be completed.

The CH and SH offer complementary ways of bringing about coherence in team functioning. The stable CH leader pulls the group together: through his ability to find each member an appropriate role in the team, he acts as a unifier in the pursuit of common objectives. The over-reactive SH leader on the other hand sets out in the opposite direction: he is there to change the point of equilibrium, to challenge, to disturb, to goad into action, enabling the group to escape from the rut into which it may well have fallen. CH and SH leaders cannot operate comfortably within the same team unless one succeeds in suppressing himself or switching to an alternative role for which he may also be equipped. Yet a group may need both members at different times.

The same potential for counterbalance is evident with our two idea-makers, but here the potential for conflict is not so sharp. The PL is usually happy enough to sit in a corner devising his own particular set of plans and formulations while the RI goes off exploring. The inward, intensive thinking approach to problem-solving is almost the opposite side of the coin from the process of finding and developing ideas through a network of personal contacts and encounters. In a sense the two sides of the coin can scarcely come face to face! Nevertheless the CH will need to bring the PL and RI together when the full range of options with which the team is faced need to be considered. Only then will the possibility of competition exist. Up to then the preferred and contrasting styles of the PL and RI result in physical separation so that neither interferes with nor impinges on the other.

MISSING TEAM-ROLES

A team that can draw on an ideal CW, CH, SH, PL and RI might seem well equipped to cope with all the vicissitudes that the future can offer; for such a team is well equipped in terms of leadership, ideas and capacity for action. In fact the balance is less complete than appears at first sight. It is quite likely that the PL and RI will present ideas to the team that are incompatible with one another and to which each is equally committed. Indeed it is not uncommon for two adversaries, each with good ideas that neither can press home successfully, to accept a compromise by backing an inferior idea advanced by a third party. Ideas are not always accepted on the basis of merit. All manner of political, personal and emotional factors enter the field to detract from a team's creative assets.

It might be thought that the task of sorting out the best ideas should fall to the team leader. This is not so because, as we have seen earlier, the team leader in terms of mental ability is very likely to be no more than average and he is not a natural "opposite" to the ideas man. The evaluation of competing proposals calls for a person who possesses a high level of mental ability combined with disinterested detachment. From time to time such a person came to the fore at critical moments in the EME to act in this new and distinctive role. We christened him – the Monitor-Evaluator (ME).

Monitor-Evaluator

What observers recorded was the emergence of one member of a team who, as often as not, had not figured very prominently until a crucial decision had to be made. A brilliant PL or an enthusiastic RI may be valued members of a group but they are seldom the best people to judge the merits of any idea they are canvassing. Nor are most other members of a team. One way or another they are too respectful or too awestruck by a particular member or they lack the sharpness of mind to find the critical flaw in an argument. The newcomer could fill the void. Intellectually, the ME was the only person who could hold his own in debate with a PL; and could cause the PL to change his standpoint and retain his respect in so doing.

By examining the test scores of those individuals who filled this role and by observing closely their behaviour, we were able to provide a detailed picture of what the ME looked like and so to build up a role specification. In the first place the ME was a high scorer in the Critical Thinking Appraisal, doing especially well in the final section of the test that deals with controversial arguments. In other words the soundness of his judgements was not disturbed by the introduction of emotionally loaded material designed to play on prejudice.

The ME emerged from the test as a serious-minded, prudent fellow with a built-in immunity from enthusiasm. He would be slow in making up his mind, always preferring to think things over. His real asset was a capacity for making shrewd judgements that took all factors into account. He would pride himself on never being wrong but he would stake no claim towards originality or imagination. On the construct analysis of the PPQ he emerged as having a significantly low achieve- ment orientation. We might describe him therefore as a man with low drive. In due course we came to realize that this failing conferred an advantage. Drive interferes with judgement: true impartiality is best served by a total lack of commitment.

To the outsider the ME may appear as rather dry, boring and some- times overcritical. Many people in meeting MEs are surprised that they have ever become managers. Nevertheless many occupy strategic posts in commerce or industry and thrive in high level appointments, especially in Head Offices. In some jobs success or failure hinges on a relatively small number of big crunch decisions. This is the ideal territory for an ME, for the man who is never wrong is the one who scores in the end.

Visions of the ME style of managing are brought home to me in a personal way when I reflect on experiences in a long established institution which I used to visit regularly in the City of London. The purpose of my visits was to introduce new methods of handling the operational side of the business in a somewhat conservative environment with a traditional way of doing things. The manager, known as the master, had the cautious qualities and characteristics that might have been expected in someone holding that particular office. This did not detract from the fact that he was a man of high ability with a deep and extensive knowledge of his subject, ever conscious of the need for change if a rational case for change could ever be made out.

The agenda for our meetings was strictly limited. We usually had only one item to discuss. The single problem would be one on which we had both done our respective preparations before we met. In effect analysis of the problem would usually leave us with about four options on which we could proceed once we had committed ourselves to a particular line of action.

We would meet first thing in the morning. Each option would be discussed as though it had equal merits with any other. We would ruminate over each proposal. There was no conceivable objection that would be overlooked, yet even the least promising option at that stage could not be dismissed out of hand. In due course we would run short of arguments and counter-arguments and conversation would lag to reach at times vanishing point. No telephone calls or casual callers would interrupt the silence for unlike most managers, the master would ensure that we were free from disturbance. Occasionally a knock would be heard at the door but this was never answered. A queue of people sometimes formed outside, quaintly hopeful of eventual admission, past which only one privileged person would proceed unchallenged – the cockney tea-lady whose smiling maternal presence was guaranteed for mid-morning. After her departure we would be back to re-examining the four options to which perhaps a fifth might be added before being eventually withdrawn. A long-anticipated lunch would provide at last a change of topic which then became as open-ended and as far-ranging as the earlier conversation had been restricted. After this one hour intermission we would return to our office for a new look, if that was possible, at the familiar options. By mid-afternoon a final decision would be reached and the necessary steps taken to turn that decision into action. The office door would then be opened and the patience of any remaining morning visitors would be rewarded.

A phenomenon is sometimes better comprehended by considering its opposite. A ME style of management is exactly what seat-of-the-pants management is not. "S-O-P" management generates for any given period of time a relatively large number of decisions; these are mainly of the instantly made variety and the risk is cheerfully taken that some are likely to be wide of the mark. By contrast ME management over the same stretch of time will generate very few decisions but it is almost certain that any decisions that are taken will be the right ones.

While the personality characteristics of a ME do not suggest a typical team person, nonetheless an ME often fits very comfortably into a team, especially if his role is clear both to himself and to others. The slowness of the team in moving to decisions is not a feature that will aggravate him, indeed it provides him with an opportunity to come into his element. Ideally he, rather than the Chairman, should be arbiter of decision making within the group. The more numerous the suggestions on offer and the more complex the decision-making process the more important his role becomes as a specialist who can replace the need for consensus.

Team Worker

Inevitably with such important but fine distinctions between the team-roles of members, many hazards arise in getting a group of diverse people to work together effectively even with a really capable Chairman. For one thing, people are often disinclined to accept the team-role for which they may be best fitted. Somebody else's team-role presents irresistible attractions. Thus an ME, especially one slow to respond, can be squeezed out of his potential contribution by more ebullient individuals, all anxious to put on record their own verdicts and judgements. In the same way, a shy but highly creative PL may be shut out by others of lower ability, anxious to give full rein to their own ideas. The danger in many groups is that individuals strive competitively to make their voice heard on any matter that comes up; no one is interested in heeding anyone else.

While members of some *companies* were very prone to display this behaviour there were occasions when a single member would stand out as the exception. Occasionally such a person would save the day. A helpful intervention would avert potential friction and enable difficult characters in the team to use their skills to positive ends. Anyone who possesses a talent of this sort has a special part to play in making a team successful, especially when it contains one or more individuals with outstanding talent but who are unable to work with colleagues.

In due course we came to recognize the need for a team-role in this area. We enlisted the help of our observers in the EME to identify individuals who had skill in listening to others and coping with awkward people, and who exercised a favourable influence on team spirit by placing group objectives above self-interest.

One sample of people who fell into this team-role – on which we soon conferred the title of Team Worker (TW) – yielded a set of revealing psychometric test scores. The TW was found to have the sociability scores commonly associated with extroverts but the low dominance scores of the introverts. The TW emerged as a trusting and sensitive personality with constructs on the PPQ test showing a strong interest in people, especially in human interaction and communication.

Some managers expressed disappointment when they found themselves dubbed TW on the basis of the various methods of assessment that we developed to establish a person's ideal team-role. It was hard for them to envisage a TW in anything other than a support job. There was genuine surprise that TWs were not uncommonly found amongst top managers on the evidence of both their psychometric test scores and their behaviour as perceived by colleagues. Environments which are dominated by Shaper-type line managers sometimes create a climate in which the diplomatic and perceptive skills of the TW become real assets, especially where an authoritarian and conflict-ridden managerial regime has run into trouble. Thus the TW manager, seen as a threat to no one and as a benefit to the group interest, is favoured by his peers as the man they would most be prepared to serve under.

> A good example of a TW top manager I encountered in the industrial world was also, as it happened, the first person to invite me to help in reconstructing an industrial team. It is entirely in keeping that such a person should have been interested in pioneering teamwork. As a director in charge of research and development in a large industrial organization he was beset with a familiar problem: an occasional project would produce an immense commercial pay-off, while many projects had very little to show for the large sums of money they consumed. That was held as being largely unavoidable. What was disturbing, however, was to find a project team with a long history of solid work and investigation being overtaken by a smaller firm that had obviously invested far less in the same project area. There seemed a possibility here of some imbalance or weakness in the long-established project team. And so it proved. Over a period of time the director made steady headway in a very controversial area in moving his personnel around in such a way that their weaknesses were not exposed and they contributed from their strengths. His personal management style was non-provocative, non-threatening but persuasive. In meetings with his managers he talked a good deal less than is normally expected of a "boss" and listened more. Other managers followed suit by talking less too. Less noise and more message characterized any meeting at which he presided.
>
> His style was distinctive too in informal situations. The director was always being consulted by others. He was regarded as a man with rare skills as a coach and tutor by graduates at junior levels of the hierarchy. At the most senior levels he was a confidant of one or two managers commonly regarded as unapproachable. In consequence he was seen as a man of influence. The position that he had reached clearly owed much to the way in which he had perfected his particular style of managing to take account both of the needs of situations and his own personality and capabilities.

TWs seem to have a lubricating effect on teams. Morale is better and people seem to co-operate more when they are present. Some groups are bound to contain awkward members. When that occurs one or more TWs can exercise a subtle influence in averting potential conflict and helping to make the task of whoever is formally chairing the meeting a much easier one.

Completer-Finisher

So far, we have found the range of useful people in teams to cover seven team-roles. To these an eighth and final one can be added, the Completer-Finisher (CF) or Completer for short. The ability to finalize anything that is started and to do so with thoroughness is a quality important for every undertaking. Unfortunately this personal quality is one that seems to be in short supply. To add to the difficulty the quality is not easy to discern when a candidate is being interviewed as part of the selection process for jobs. Enthusiasm to get things moving may easily be detected but the ability to finish things off once started is much less evident. There are many able people who are good to a greater or lesser degree at practically everything but who are almost pathological when it comes to being able to complete anything they start.

> If a team-role can be understood by considering those human deficiencies which create a need for it, then a good example came our way when we had occasion to run a graduate induction programme for a national airline. We had been asked to introduce the concept of management team-roles to sixteen graduates recruited from an original field of 300 screened applicants. Since the applicants had been submitted to a battery of tests including measures of mental ability, the sixteen selected candidates showed themselves impressively bright during the seminar, as might be expected. The tests we gave them were however related to personal characteristics indicating likely affinity or lack of affinity for the given team-roles. My colleague Bill Hartston and I then interviewed each of the course members to discuss the implication of their test scores. Some of the course members were low in Completer team-role score and this was particularly so in the case of one young lady. When Hartston discreetly pointed out the facts to her, she hastened to agree, observing, "I wonder if that would tie up with the fact that I have been knitting myself a jumper for nine years; it is still unfinished."

What our studies had discovered was that poor finishing qualities were associated with individuals who tended to have a cavalier attitude to detail and a low regard for obligations. The lack of a Completer Finisher emerged as a common reason for teams that looked within certain grasp of their goals failing at the very last hurdle. It was a typical experience in the Henley management game to find small computational errors upsetting a well-conceived operational strategy. In the exercise that played a central part in the team-building seminars, *companies* sometimes missed key auctions and tenders by late attendance often of no more than a few vital seconds. If a battle was lost for a horse and the horse for a shoe and the shoe for a nail, then the old proverb seemed to have lost none of its relevance. Small mishaps can spell grave misfortune. Attention to detail is not a trivial matter. Someone with a capacity for relentless followthrough is a real asset in any team.

Our experiences had many counterparts in the industrial world, especially in the launching of new products and models. Often a product is well conceived but fails to establish its share in the market due to some early reverse from which it never recovers. The launching team may be well equipped with enthusiasts amongst its designers, marketeers and salesmen most of whom look forward eagerly to D-day. What tends to be lacking is someone prepared to hold things back until all the necessary tests, checks and safeguards have been completed and the product can be announced as truly ready to go. Sometimes the tests reveal that the product is not in fact a runner and should be scrapped or redesigned. Market research or independent laboratory testing may provide the unwelcome news but news that may save a company from ruin.

A good illustration of the need for a Completer arose during a period in which I ran seminars on Total Quality Control for the British Institute of Management on whose behalf I published a paper on Quality Calamities. During the course of this work I was able to obtain information on 121 Quality Calamities (defined as simple quality-related incidents that resulted in a large financial loss). The underlying causes of those calamities were studied and at the forefront came lack of proving (whether of new designs, materials or processes), accounting for 36% of all cases. A typical instance of a large calamity was provided by a company manufacturing rubber thread by a continuous process which involved extruding latex into acetic acid and drawing it through a casing oven to emerge, in its finished state, ready for covering with yarn. As the price of natural rubber increased, the company found itself impelled to search for alternative materials. An American company, with which it had associations, had just launched a new synthetic rubber thread. This was a good deal cheaper. Moreover, advantages were claimed for some of its physical properties. Negotiations began and the British team soon committed itself to take up the licence for the UK. Production was switched from natural to synthetic rubber thread and customers were persuaded that they would enjoy a number of benefits. In their haste to accept the deal the British company omitted to submit the new rubber to the exhaustive range of tests that their well-equipped technical laboratory could provide. One of these tests covered accelerated ageing. In the event the new rubber was found to have poor ageing properties which made it unsuitable for its main market outlet. Claims from customers for damages resulted and in the end the whole venture had to be abandoned with consequential losses estimated to exceed two million pounds. There had been nothing at fault with the detailed technical information furnished by the American company. It was just that one physical property was not mentioned. No one in the British management team had thought it worthwhile to submit the product to a total check.

It requires a manager with a particular attitude of mind to plan ahead, to ensure that nothing is overlooked and that all detailed plans have been completed to satisfaction. We therefore set out to look for CF managers who displayed this particular facility in our experimental situations. They were not easy to find for many managers confessed to losing interest in a new idea once all the exciting new features had been explored. Yet success is seldom easily earned and a certain sense of perfectionism is indispensable for achievement. In time we reached the view that Completer managers tended to fight shy of training and education courses but they were not uncommon when one got into the heart of successful enterprises.

Self-introduction was the means by which one notable Completer crossed my path when the Chairman of an international trust sent me a letter out of the blue containing the following paragraph: "To delegate to people one has to trust them to do things reasonably in the style one prefers, I believe. Thus I want devices to help me find people who share a particular kink that I have. Could this just be nonsense?"

The writer of the letter was Ernest Cobb who was to emerge as a Completer/Plant. (The most successful Completers in management often have a strong back-up team-role either as Plant or Monitor-Evaluator.)

Ernest Cobb was the son of a leading figure in the world of international politics and diplomacy. Cobb was reluctant to follow his father's urges to pursue a financial career and had felt instead that he would like to do something worthwhile with his inherited money in the context of the major problems facing the world. One day he threw up his work on Wall Street and moved to India to study and address himself to the problems of the population explosion. There he remained for some years in a vain attempt to grapple with the problems at a practical level. Finally he returned to the West convinced that successful applied work could only follow from the harnessing of technical knowledge. He considered he would have to rationalize the information flow in this field and accordingly set up an organization and a journal for this purpose. For three years he worked unpaid, with three assistants, compiling a monthly bibliography and setting up a service and a company that was to become financially self-supporting. "The type of work appealed to me. It was the old stamp collecting interest again. I like tidying up loose ends and I am compulsive about getting things done." During this period he became a Trustee of a Research Trust in the field and the experience enabled him to see the importance of working in teams (usually ten or more people) to achieve some of the objectives that had always inspired him. He now began to utilize a skill that he had always had with gadgetry. Setting up his own workshop – which on inspection proved to be immaculately laid out – he developed with his colleagues invention after invention, the products of which are now used in hospitals in many countries. He is now the Chairman of the Trust, having given up his duties with his old Company after twelve years. "Since it is now so well established that it runs itself."

Ernest Cobb seems to have a need to finish anything he starts. When he recounts what he considers his failures in life he blames his poor judgement and declares: "The objectives were not achievable and I held on too long" . . . The Completer's failures and successes are all part of the same characteristic.

By taking good examples of the CF type of manager we were able to establish a set of psychometric test scores which gave the test correlates of the behaviour pattern. What these scores tended to reveal was that CF managers though prone to anxiety were high in self-control and self-discipline. Their peers in their syndicates and *companies* seldom saw them as anxious, even veering in the other direction and regarding them as calm and unflappable. The CF manager tended to be introverted rather than extroverted. He seemed to look for and absorb stress, although it would take its toll sometimes in physical terms. In due course we came to interpret an ulcer as a promising sign of the ideal CF manager! On the construct analysis of the PPQ the CF manager tended to favour steady effort, survival, consistency and was less interested in the glamour of spectacular success.

The CF style of management, along with CW and TW styles, tends to be underrated and managers need persuasion that this style is not uncommon amongst successful top managers. Inevitably distortions arise in the public mind about the characteristics of top management. Managers in the news tend naturally to be those of more flamboyant disposition and are therefore accepted as generally representative of the genus. But behind the scenes many top managers differ from the stereotype of the big businessman. Their success is founded on the more sterling qualities of character and discipline that underline their capacity for hard, effective work. They finish everything they start and they are reluctant to undertake anything where there are doubts about being able to see it through. Time is never wasted when a CF manager becomes a member of a team; ideally his qualities need to be widened and socialized. He is concerned not merely with finishing for himself but for the wider group. Good finishing is a valued art and the person who makes his or her mark in this area is quickly recognized and appreciated by his colleagues.

CONCLUSION

The eight types of people identified as useful to have in teams form our comprehensive list. After half a decade of industrial experience in composing teams we could not find any other useful team-role to add. This does not mean that people may not be welcome in teams for their personal qualities, like a sense of humour, or for their technical knowledge, as befits a specialist. It is that such people cannot take up any generalizable team-role in which they would have definite responsibilities. Good examples of our eight types would prove adequate for any challenge, although not all eight team-roles are necessarily needed.

The procedure for assessing each person in terms of the team which he might best enter was to establish from our psychometric test predictors the two roles for which that person might best be suited – the first role being his most dominant one and the second his best back-up. Hence ME/CF would apply to a person whose main characteristic was that he was clever and had a capacity for impartial judgement but who was also the sort of person who would not be happy with any loose ends that might be left around. RI/TW would indicate an extroverted person who loved exploring new ideas and who communicated and related easily and well with others.

The value of particular team-roles could be demonstrated by constructing teams that were deficient in some· given team-role. Although those teams might succeed in capitalizing on their collective strength, any shortcoming in performance usually reflected the fault inherent in their team composition.

The strengths and weaknesses of teams, according to their team composition, will be considered in the next two chapters. Already we have, by way of introduction, established a few basic propositions.

The useful people to have in teams are those who possess strengths or characteristics which serve a need without duplicating those already there. Teams are a question of balance. What is needed is not well-balanced individuals but individuals who balance well with one another. In that way, human frailties can be underpinned and strengths used to full advantage.

USEFUL PEOPLE TO HAVE IN TEAMS

Type	Symbol	Typical Features	Positive Qualities	Allowable Weaknesses
Company Worker	CW	Conservative, dutiful, predictable.	Organizing ability, practical common sense, hard-working, self-discipline.	Lack of flexibility, unresponsiveness to unproven ideas.
Chairman	CH	Calm, self-confident controlled.	A capacity for treating and welcoming all potential contributors on their merits and without prejudice. A strong sense of objectives.	No more than ordinary in terms of intellect or creative ability.
Shaper	SH	Highly strung, outgoing, dynamic.	Drive and a readiness to challenge inertia, ineffectiveness, complacency or self-deception.	Proneness to provocation, irritation and impatience.
Plant	PL	Individualistic, serious-minded, unorthodox.	Genius, imagination, intellect, knowledge.	Up in the clouds, inclined to disregard practical details or protocol.
Resource Investigator	RI	Extroverted, enthusiastic, curious, communicative.	A capacity for contacting people and exploring anything new. An ability to respond to challenge.	Liable to lose interest once the initial fascination has passed.
Monitor-Evaluator	ME	Sober, unemotional, prudent.	Judgement, discretion, hard-headedness.	Lacks inspiration or the ability to motivate others.
Team Worker	TW	Socially orientated, rather mild, sensitive.	An ability to respond to people and to situations, and to promote team spirit.	Indecisiveness at moments of crisis.
Completer-Finisher	CF	Painstaking, orderly, conscientious, anxious.	A capacity for follow-through. Perfectionism.	A tendency to worry about small things. A reluctance to "let go".

7: Unsuccessful Teams

Our experimental work in building teams to various design specifications and then testing them out in competitive situations gave us the opportunity to look at teams which might otherwise never have come into being. To be allowed to compose a team of deliberately poor design is a rare privilege. No manager would ever set about or be allowed to set about such a task. The virtue of studying a badly composed team is that it furnishes valuable information about what can go wrong. Basic principles can be established and cause and effect examined. Knowing what to avoid can become one of the arts in good design.

Before we examine the characteristics of unsuccessful teams a few words might be said about the problem of carrying out this particular investigation. Losing teams create more embarrassment for their members than winning teams; and the difficulties were greater in the EME than in Teamopoly. The latter exercise offered the advantage of being under our own control and we were aided by the fact that the participants had come to learn about team-building and nothing more. The strain of failing can be endured provided it does not last too long.

Members of the newly formed *companies* would convene for a drink before lunch and five hours later by the time dinner was due the exercise was finished. Victors and vanquished toasted their success or drowned their sorrows accordingly. Later that evening they went off on their separate paths to conduct their inquests and prepare their presentations for the following day. For the most part, the *companies* that finished last accepted their reverse in good humour. Whether failure reflected the design, usually deliberate in the construction of the team or a failure to use the resources of the team in the best way, there were lessons to be learned. That, after all, was the reason they were attending the seminar.

The Henley EME was a different proposition. In the first place the game extended over a longer time span; at the beginning of our experiments it occupied one period every day, lasting in all one week. Secondly, team-building was not the reason for the management game, although it was embraced within it. The main purpose of the EME was to make managers more aware of "the quantitative basis of decision-making". The game occupied but a fraction of the ten-week course, the duration of which indicated the scale of investment that a firm or institution was making in the development of the manager chosen to go to Henley. Naturally the career expectations of Henley members were commensurate with the length of the course. The management game furnished them with the first real opportunity to test their ambitions by pitting themselves against others in a competitive setting. In such circumstances losing was not a matter to be taken lightly. In Teamopoly we could concoct bad teams with devilish cunning and delight and with impunity. At Henley it was a different matter. We were under pressure not to construct wholly bad teams and it was considered politically desirable that every *company* should be given a reasonable chance of winning. Our poor designs had therefore to be watered down so that they became less extreme examples of the type. Yet in spite of their restrictions basically the same patterns emerged in both our management exercises.

The characteristic features of unsuccessful teams were judged by scrutinizing the design of *companies* that tended to finish last, that usually fell into the bottom half of the results table and never won. This strict criterion meant that we had to remove Apollo teams from our well-defined group of ineffective teams. An occasional Apollo team did win. Their general results were poor but failure was not inevitable. By contrast some teams were so poorly constructed that they never overcame the disadvantage rendered by their composition.

MORALE – A MARGINAL FACTOR

After collecting our sample of consistently unsuccessful teams we set about examining the observer records of their performance in the EME or our own notes in the case of Teamopoly. We were able to draw up a league of demerit, having at its head the feature of team design most certain to ensure failure. But we discovered one interesting point. Unsuccessful teams do not necessarily suffer from poor morale or poor apparent team work. Poor morale may reveal itself – and it usually did – as a consequence of failure or of diminishing fortunes but it should not be seen as its cause. Some of the *companies* finishing with abysmal results started out as happy teams: even at the end members sometimes commented on how much they had enjoyed working with one another. "They went down smiling" was a typical comment by onlookers. Intense personal conflicts between members did arise in a number of *companies* but these conflicts did not necessarily presage poor results. In other words the relationship between morale and results at the bottom end of the scale seemed a tenuous one.

MENTAL ABILITY – A CRITICAL FACTOR

Because of the sensitive nature of the subject it is easier to report on the characteristics of "worst team design" in this book than it was at the time, when running seminars or management games. This was certainly the case with the leading predictor of poor team results which was uniformly low scoring on the measures of mental ability. Even one good scorer could make all the difference to the outcome, especially if he was either a good Plant or a good Monitor Evaluator. The lesson is that every management team needs to have within it one person, at least, who is clever, whether in an analytical or a creative sense. Unless there is someone effective in the sort of team-role that a clever person carves out for himself, that company will be heading for trouble.

This generalization is a fair working hypothesis applicable to virtually every situation in which a management group holds major responsibilities. The principle is seldom stated as boldly as it has been here, but empirically it seems to be followed in practice by the more successful industrial and commercial enterprises. The recruitment of graduates, however irrelevant their academic discipline, is the uncomplicated way in which firms ensure that they secure their requisite share of managers with good mental ability. Sophisticated companies go a good deal further than this, as we shall see in our next chapter. The assessment of mental ability has become a standard procedure in the search for potential managers.

The failure on the part of companies to obtain an adequate proportion of managers with good mental ability can scarcely be due to a conscious search for managers of low intelligence. That unintended result is simply a by-product of overvaluing a particular factor in recruitment that is found to have a negative association with mental ability.

Negative Selection

Here it is useful to consider the concept of *negative selection*. This term refers to a recruitment process that, while being designed to achieve one intended effect, becomes more important for its unintended effects in filtering out the very candidates of which the company stands in need. A typical example is where a company in a state of continuous decline looks for a general manager capable of causing its fortunes to recover but insists that the advertised salary is kept in line with the already depressed salaries of its current senior executives. This recruitment arrangement is ideally, though unintentionally, designed to exclude just the sort of general manager who would best fit the bill.

An instance of *negative selection* in the context of mental ability is well illustrated by the following case of a company that has earned itself a reputation for unsuccess.

Multigate is a large engineering group mainly centred on the Midlands. Although the company grew as a result of mergers to become the conglomerate that it is today many of its characteristics echo the views and values of its now deceased but not forgotten founder. Bert Rawlings was a self-taught engineer with drive and vision, who had started in business on his own account at a very early age. He was a practical man in both its positive and its more restrictive senses. On the one hand he had a genius for making things work while on the other he had a dislike, or even contempt, for anything he considered theoretical. This distinction was of no particular importance so long as he himself worked closely with those who held key executive positions in his company and he could assess personally the competence of his colleagues. The bond of shared experiences opened up the avenues of communication. But he was much more ill-at-ease when he had to confer with the men whose backgrounds differed from his own and who had to be judged by their arguments and advice rather than by what he saw as any real evidence of their practical competence.

As Bert Rawlings's company grew in size he endeavoured to surround himself with those who had come up the hard way and with whose thinking and attitudes he felt most at home. His choice fell largely upon apprentice trained engineers. Through internal promotion they were appointed to the senior positions in the company while outsiders were rigorously excluded and graduate recruitment was non-existent. Had Bert endeavoured to broaden his appointees through further education and training there might have been something to be said for this policy. But Bert's company was conspicuous by its abstention from all the various facilities and courses that were on offer for the development of managers. After Bert's death the company continued to grow on a rising market and in the search for economies of scale merging with other companies in the process. Nevertheless on the personnel front the old traditions remained. Bert Rawlings's men were the cast from which Multigate managers were drawn.

The first downturn in the market had a particularly severe effect on the fortunes of Multigate. The market recovered, then oscillated but the company was now set on a downward path. In the face of impending financial collapse one new chief executive followed another. Eventually Multigate underwent a change of ownership and then started recruiting graduates but the culture was unreceptive and no real change of character resulted until eventually that formidable outsider Spikey Smart was brought in on a rescue mission.

New managers usually bring about changes in the top management team. It had happened before in Multigate and in this regard Spikey Smart was following precedent. But this time there was a difference. The newcomer boldy required those executives he had inherited in responsible positions to be "assessed" and as part of this process arranged that they should take intelligence tests. The move was not well received by those concerned. But Smart got his way. In the event the distribution of scores amongst Multigate executives compared unfavourably with those of executive populations in other branches of industry. Here was further backing for those executive changes that Smart now felt impelled to make.

Whether Smart had consciously suspected it or not, the personnel policy begun by Bert Rawlings was an instance of *negative selection* based on intelligence. In other words a person of very high intelligence would have been unlikely to have ended up as one of Bert Rawlings's executives. The reason was straightforward enough. In the founder's day apprentice engineers were recruited overwhelmingly from those who left school at an early age. With few exceptions they were drawn from the streams of lower educational ability in the school. The system of sorting pupils into the type of school which the educational authorities considered suitable for their abilities depended upon an assessment at a critical age. Intelligence tests played a part in this examination. Hence those who performed poorly in these tests were more likely to get into the stream from which apprentice engineers – and the eventual Multigate executives – were recruited.

The Multigate example is a reminder of one of the strongest predictors, under experimental results, of factors associated with company failure. A general set of poor or indifferent scores on mental ability in the management team seems to preclude the chances of eventual success. If a single factor had to be singled out as posing the gravest risk, this might be the one to select.

PERSONALITY

Although mental ability usually has a fair spread amongst the executives of most firms, yet firms differ a good deal from one another in their cultural milieu. This is seldom due to any isolated cause. The explanation is more complex and has something to do with the culture of the firm. The variations in culture give firms different personalities. Some firms are typically extrovert, being generally social and outward-looking; they thrive on new stimulus but are inclined to be casual when it comes to follow-through. Other firms seemingly have introvert personalities; they are self-sustaining and inclined to withdraw into themselves, pursuing internally generated goals with a certain relentlessness. Again the culture becomes a moulding force creating a type of collective personality. Individual executives whose private personalities contrast with the personality of the firm usually end up acting in accordance with the cultural norm which the firm engenders.

The concept of a firm's personality is worth considering in a general way in relation to the observations of the *companies* experimentally composed according to personality and discussed in Chapter Three. Anxious Introvert *companies* tended to perform poorly. Members of AI *companies* were often specialists who had risen through their speciality into management. In spite of their advancement they were still prone to act like specialists, failing to take a rounded view of the problems confronting them.

Some firms in the high technology field appear to have a typical AI culture. The greater role and say which specialists have in them result in a pattern of activities that are reminiscent of the general behaviour of AI *companies* in the EME. A single-minded concentration on particular ends can give rise in practice to what M. F. Woods of the University of Bradford's Management Centre has called the Concorde Syndrome. Woods's letter to *The Guardian* in which he expands on this danger is worth quoting in full.

> One factor seems to have been omitted from the discussion on the Finniston report on engineering. I would term this factor the Concorde Syndrome.
> British industry – in direct contrast to Germany and Japan – goes for the large spectacular project. In the public sector I can list Princess, Brabazon, TSR 2, Bevercotes (NCB Automated Pit), Magnox, AGR, etc . . .
> The examples in the private sector are less publicised but no less damaging – the RB 211 is classic. We go for huge "quantum leap" projects with high risk and ignore the personally boring, but commercially rewarding, business of doing what we already know better, planned progression into well researched market driven areas. In fact, we may be accused of lack of professionalism.
> The Concorde Syndrome is due to unbalance – of risk, but, most importantly, of management teams. An engineer or a marketing man or a chemist, is allowed to run away with a project and the remainder of the skills are ignored.
> To press the case for the engineer will not help the Concorde Syndrome or reduce its gross attrition of our material wealth. Getting the specialist into professional management teams is a different matter altogether.

Team-roles act of course as a brake on runaway specialists.

COMPOSITION OF UNSUCCESSFUL TEAMS

When it comes to considering what can be done about the problem, ineffective management teams can be classified as falling into two types. There are those which are products of the culture so that the faults of the management team epitomize the faults to which the firm as a whole has long been subject. In such cases changes in the management team may have only marginal effects. The second type of ineffective team has no deeply rooted causes but is linked with an unfortunate combination of characters. Remedial action may not be easy as socially contentious issues are involved, subtle factors are operating, and diagnosis is not obvious.

Typical instances of the latter type of ineffective team occur where obstacles prevent individuals finding their preferred team-role. This can be true for any team-role. It can be true too for individuals who are good examples of the team-role type. The following companies illustrate poor design combinations associated with an otherwise useful person.

A Chairman along with two dominant Shapers both above average in mental ability. (The CH will almost certainly fail to get the job of Chairman.)

A Plant in a company with another Plant, more dominant but less creative, and no good candidate to take the chair. (The PL will be inhibited and will probably make no creative contribution at all.)

A Monitor-Evaluator with no Plant and surrounded by Team Workers and Company Workers of highly stable disposition and good mental ability. (The team is likely to generate a climate of solid orderly working and not foresee any need to evaluate alternative strategies or ideas.)

A Company Worker in a team of Company Workers with no Plant and no Resource Investigator. (The company will lack direction and the organizers will not have much to organize.)

A Team Worker working with Team Workers, Company Workers and Completers but no Resource Investigator, Plant, Shaper or Chairman. (A happy, conscientious company will be overanxious to reach agreement so that the presence of another TW merely adds to the euphoria.)

A Shaper working with another Shaper, highly dominant and of low mental ability, a Superplant, anxious and recessive, plus two or more Company Workers. (The SH will find that any display of drive and energy on his part is likely to increase provocation and aggravation and disturb further an already unbalanced team).

A Resource Investigator with other Resource Investigators and Plants but no Team Workers, Completers, Monitor-Evaluators or Chairman. (A formula for a talking shop in which no one listens, follows up any of the points, or makes any decisions about what to do.)

A Completer with Monitor-Evaluators and Company Workers but no Resource Investigator, Plant or Shaper. (The CF if he intervenes at all will probably only help an already slow-moving company to get bogged down in detail.)

All these cases exemplify someone who can potentially make a valuable contribution to a team but who is unlikely to do so. His natural team-role will be blocked either by the apparent lack of need for it or by the presence of competing persons. That does not mean that his team-role will be enacted by another. Where too many cooks spoil the broth it is probably the case that no one cook succeeds in doing much of the cooking. Equally the cooking can be obstructed by having other people around who only serve to get in the way.

The firm that in real life is faced with this problem need not be too pessimistic about its prospects. Some recombination of people may yet produce an effective team. A Managing Director of a large group once expressed the remedy with a neat turn of phrase: "If things are not working out, you just shake the bag." Even random rearrangements are capable of producing improved results.

TEAM MEMBERS WITH NO TEAM-ROLE

Badly composed *companies* in our experimental teams usually featured team-role clashes, overlaps or voids. In the case of Teamopoly we deliberately set about making these poor mixes. In that way managers became more aware of the nature of the problems poor team design could bring about. Whether a manager acquiesced in the problems confronting him or struggled to get more out of the team by adjusting his own team-role, there were lessons to be learned.

We now come to a more personalized factor that often attaches itself to the ineffective team; this is the presence within it of a member or members who can be counted as liabilities rather than assets. This does not mean that the team design is basically at fault. It is simply that some individuals do not fit at all well into *any* team, detracting from a team's potential rather than adding materially to it. For about thirty per cent of managers we tested we could find no appropriate team-role. These indefinite characters who were not without ability contained a higher incidence of problem people than we would expect to find in any cross-section of managers. Here are three typical examples.

Mr. Black is a man whose test scores suggest high mental ability although he is clearly not creative. His cleverness, however, is not easily put to advantage because as part of his highly extrovert tendencies he reacts to everything in a highly spontaneous way. He talks first and thinks afterwards. This rules him out as a Monitor-Evaluator and he cannot make a Plant. His self-control scores in the Personality Inventory are low and his constructs show a good deal of egocentricity. There is no prospect that he can make a Company Worker or a Chairman as he lacks the basic self-discipline. He is not social enough to be a Resource Investigator or a Team Worker and he lacks the urgency of a Completer or a Shaper. Nevertheless because he is exuberant and mentally sharp he is likely to exert a major influence on how the team operates. The danger is that he will spoil a team's chances and unintentionally stop others emerging in their best team-role.

Mr. Towers is a man of low mental ability but very high dominance and self-confidence. He is too cavalier in his approach to make a Shaper and his constructs on the PPQ are rather more orientated towards Justice than Achievement. Hence he is preoccupied with the rights and wrongs of the world rather than getting things done. He is full of hope while things go well. But once his team drifts into difficulties he is more interested in finding excuses than with putting things right.

Mr. Sittman has moderate mental ability and high anxiety scores. However, he has no interest in practical detail and has low scores on the Control Scales of the Personality Inventory so there is no prospect of his becoming a Completer. He is too recessive and inward-looking to make a Shaper. As soon as the team meets its first reverse he is liable to become demoralized. The other team members do not know what to make of him. If he is given responsibility he may discharge it poorly, covering up any mistakes he has made. His self doubts are apt to become obstacles to action. He gives up easily but never formally contracts out of his responsibilities. This makes it difficult for others ever to take over anything he has been doing or to recognize what has gone wrong.

Managers who are liabilities in a team pose less serious problems than those who have a certain wrecking streak. These seem to be managers with a high capacity for spontaneous action, keen wits, and a disinclination to consult others. Fortunately they are few in number but they can go a long way in industry where conditions allow them the opportunity. At an early stage in my industrial career I encountered a remarkable personality in this mould.

Ed Rushton was the Sales Manager of a company in a high technology process industry. Unlike his predecessors, he took a keen interest in what went on in the laboratory. Whenever there was the merest hint that some experimental development could have some favourable implication for sales, he would wander round the laboratory unannounced and talk to people on his own. The extent of his interest was remarkable considering that he had not been with the company for long and had no technical background. One day he was shown the results of trials with a new material by a junior laboratory worker who was somewhat lacking in caution about its virtues and prospects. Rushton seized a specimen of the material and ran from the laboratory. Later the management learned that leading customers had been told about this new breakthrough and dates for eventual production had even been mentioned. This was embarrassing as the development was at an early stage. It was even doubtful that the trial material would become a production proposition at all. Undismayed by the *faux pas* Rushton was soon forging ahead with another policy initiative of his own choosing when he was at last called to account. In the ensuing showdown Rushton departed with a golden handshake. After a short interval Rushton turned up again as the Managing Director of a major competitor. What happened in that company is uncertain but in due course "after a policy disagreement at Board level" Rushton was removed, receiving a large amount for the termination of his services. Rushton was next heard of in an entirely different field as Chairman of a conglomerate industrial holding company. After only two years in that position the appointment ended, with Rushton receiving what at that time was believed to be a UK record sum as compensation for loss of office.

Managers who fail to fit into any management team tend to move from one appointment to another. In so doing they amass a track record which facilitates a rapid rise to the top; on the other hand, managers who fit well into a top management team tend to stay put. The team-role qualities of a manager are seldom taken into account because management lacks relevant data to help them in the selection of managers or in the choosing of colleagues.

UNKNOWN ELEMENTS IN TEAMS

There were occasions in our experiments when we too lacked data about the managers who were being placed in teams. Over the years an average of between ten and fifteen per cent of members failed to take the tests. Some of these were overseas members, a little bewildered on their arrival from Africa and Asia, who, seeing that the tests were voluntary, availed themselves of the respite from the general pressure of course demands. The U.K. drop outs included some who were busy preparing a speech or report and from time to time sporting enthusiasts who found the attraction of playing squash greater than that of taking tests. But the greater number of members who declined to take the tests did so from some positive objection. They did not believe in tests; they saw them as an invasion of personal privacy; they mistrusted the assurances that the information would be treated as confidential and suspected that the results would be leaked in some way to their employers.

Placing members who did not take the tests into teams became a highly speculative business. We could only guess as to what they might be like. We could not impute to them any particular team-role. They were therefore excluded from team designs of any special interest. Instead they would land up in a rag-bag team of people who were left over from the other teams we had composed. On more than one occasion we made up teams entirely of people who had not taken the tests. But whatever arrangements were made for them they seemed to increase the accuracy of our predictions- non test-takers were strongly associated with *companies* that failed (usually finishing bottom). This was especially likely to be the result if they took up any key position of responsibility within the *company*.

We cannot be sure why individuals unwilling to volunteer for tests tended to perform less well than those who did volunteer. Was it part of a more general proneness to suspicion that was detrimental to team-work? Or could it have been that a sense of embarrassment or even guilt in not taking the tests militated against a positive approach in the exercise? There was no objective reason why they should have felt exposed. None of their colleagues knew who had taken the tests and who had not unless they themselves volunteered the information. The only consequence of substance for the non test-takers was that they did not have an interview with me to discuss their best team-role in groups. Here they were similarly placed to those whose test results did not suggest much of an affinity for any particular team-role. These individuals for the most part also turned out to be indifferent team performers.

It looks as though those with no evident team-role are at some disadvantage in comparison with those who can find one. A person with somewhat marked idiosyncrasies was often pleased to find that these had important team-role implications. A quiet, rather dry man with good analytical ability but slow to make up his mind may in the past have regretted that he was not a dynamic manager; but now, he would be relieved to find he was a classic Monitor-Evaluator. New possibilities would be opened up for him and he would strive to develop those team talents that he found latent within him.

Indefinite Team-Role Teams

Some *companies* that we composed comprised people with classic team-role profiles, while other *companies* were formed from people with indefinite team-role profiles. The members of the latter seemed less concerned about the part they could best play in a team and tended instead to gravitate towards the job which technically they knew most about.

How this worked out may best be illustrated by a condensed account from an observer report in the EME.

Five of the members arrived promptly and began looking through their notes. After a few minutes JR suggested that the first task was to elect a Chairman. JP announced that he didn't want the job in any circumstances as he was already involved in two chairs. Similar noises were made by the others. When TF walked into the room JR said jokingly: "You've got the job". TF agreed that if it would help he was ready to be Chairman. The remaining board positions were filled by people volunteering for jobs most in line with their experience; RW, Finance; JR, Marketing; JP said he was prepared to take on Production and Purchasing and he also said that PB's experience should suit him for Management Services. WG's legal background equipped him to be secretary . . . Each member of the team worked on his own or with another.

There was little planning and co-ordination work within the group and the Chairman was very passive, until the time came when the forms had to be filled in. Policies were then discussed but each person ended up by taking responsibility for decisions in his own area . . . The group seemed to work co-operatively and to be enjoying the exercise . . . There was gloom when the bad results were announced.

IMPORTANCE OF CORPORATE THOUGHT

If every manager carries out his functional responsibilities in a professional way, the company must do well – or so it is said. The facts often tell a different story, whether in a management game or within the normal operations of the firm. What fails to be taken into account is the way in which departmental objectives are capable of conflicting with one another. Any major change in one department can affect other departments. The ineffective company is the company where top managers remain locked within departmental patterns of thinking and cannot develop a corporate view.

The distorting effect of departmental thinking at top level is well illustrated by a large company that supplied components widely used in the consumer durable market. In its early days when there were few good suppliers it was dominated by Production and run by an able autocrat in a highly authoritarian style. The company was able to supply the much-needed goods and it grew rapidly. Later it lost ground as other competitors came on the scene. The autocratic Chief Executive then moved to the holding group and sales. The company now concentrated on studying and meeting its customers' needs. Large stocks of finished goods were built up and the service offered to customers gradually allowed it to acquire a semi-monopolistic position and with it high profitability. A general recession combined with structural changes in the market then coincided with the retirement of the Chief Executive. He was succeeded by a man with less general experience but a keen interest in finance. As cash flow problems began to develop massive cuts were made in the company's stocks and in the amount of money tied up in them. This produced in the short term startlingly good results. But later when the consumer durable industry which had overreacted to the recession found itself short of parts, the company was unable to respond in time. New competitors entered on to the scene to take advantage of the supply gap. The profitable semi-monopolistic position was lost and the once thriving company now found itself struggling to maintain its trading viability.

The team-role approach to management allows corporate thinking to develop and protects firms from the hazards of functional dominance. There are real dilemmas in the objectives, policies and priorities between which organizations have to choose. It is better that the issues are thrashed out in an effective but dispassionate way by the management team than that they are glossed over or that one particular manager should be allowed to dominate proceedings.

TEAM-ROLE REVERSAL

So far the pattern of ineffective management teams has been considered as a function of design faults. Enough was learned about badly composed teams in the experimental work to enable us to predict with some confidence which teams were destined to become losers. Not all failures. however, could have been forecast from the outset because some *companies* that seemed well equipped in all ways somehow managed to snatch defeat out of the jaws of victory.

These unpredictable failures were associated especially with reversals in team-role. What is meant by this is that a person who was a natural for one team-role would take another. Once such a change had been made the whole company was liable to get out of step. In one memorable instance we had placed a dynamic Shaper into a talented but rather weak *company* to give it thrust. The Shaper duly became the Chairman but then acted like the most passive type of Team Worker. The *company* finished up in bottom place. The unexpected explanation for the Shaper's behaviour was that he had recently been taken to task by someone for his excessively forthright and aggressive behaviour. Thinking he must learn the lesson he had overcompensated. It was a pity, of course, that he had not learned how to be an effective Shaper instead!

The more usual type of unexpected failure results from a poor allocation of manpower resources within the team. An ideal CH becomes the Secretary and an anxious TW is appointed Chairman. The PL does the data gathering and recording and a rather rigid CW takes over negotiation. A RI with low critical thinking takes over planning while the CF becomes responsible for developing new strategies.

Fortunately the mismatch is rarely as bad as that but even a small mismatch can rapidly bring about a reversal of fortunes.

Teams can use their internal resources to good or poor effect. The more conscious they are of where their strengths and weaknesses lie, the easier it is to adjust to that information. The lower this awareness, the greater the danger of making strategic mistakes that spring from self-delusion. Perhaps that is why *companies* with members who declined to take the tests did so badly.

8: Winning Teams

The whole world is interested in winners. An Olympic gold medallist may beat the silver medallist in a race by 0.1 of a second but the great majority of people treat the two competitors as being in different classes. It was much the same in our experimental studies where our long-standing focus on prediction as a means of testing the theory and technique of team design excited the recurring and restricted question: did you pick the winner?

Whereas many people supposed that our only object was to produce *the* winning team, in reality we were equally interested in getting right the approximate rank order of all the teams. As a task the former would have been much easier. Other teams could have been starved of the most useful people. Instead we had the more difficult task of making fine discriminations between teams. The team that we forecast as coming second had to be "quite a good team" but not so good as the team forecast as coming first.

PREDICTION

Although therefore our main concern was not to produce one winning team so much as to make a generally accurate forecast, there is something of value to be gained for the purpose of this chapter in focusing our attention on the companies that actually won. What were they like? And what have we to learn about their composition and operation?

Before we begin to answer these questions we must concede that it was more difficult to predict the team that would finish first than the one that would finish last. Experience soon taught us that a team can have such a membership that even before it convenes it has no hope of performing anything but badly. On the other hand, a team which on paper looks very good may disappoint in practice. One small unforeseen factor could spoil the otherwise promising pattern. A loss of interest for personal reasons by some key person might undermine the collective effort; the absence of one member could enforce some re-allocation of jobs that would not turn out well; or a *company* might fail to capitalize on a winning advantage through over-confidence after a runaway start. Admittedly a well-composed team has enough talent and resilience to recover from any reverse and to end up with a result that is at least respectable. But *companies* placed first in our forecast did not necessarily win though they usually occupied one of the first three places and none ever finished bottom.

A composite picture of the typical *company* that figured most prominently at the top of the results table can now be built up. Of the various contributing factors, the most positive indicators were the attributes of the person in the Chair, the existence of a good Plant, a spread in mental abilities, a spread also in personal attributes laying the foundation for different team-role capabilities, a distribution in the responsibilities of members to match their different capabilities, and finally, an adjustment to the realization of imbalance. These points, some of which have been alluded to earlier, now seem worth enlarging upon.

1. *The Person in the Chair*

Here it proved important that there should be an affinity between the measured personal attributes of the person in the Chair and the good Chairman profile that our research had identified (see Chapter Five). This formula portrayed the successful Chairman as a patient but commanding figure who generated trust and who looked for and knew how to use ability. He would not dominate proceedings but he knew when to pull matters together if a critical decision had to be reached or a meeting had to close. In practice he always worked with, rather than against, the most talented contributors to the group.

2. *The Existence of One Strong Plant in the Group*

Winning *companies* were characterized by the inclusion of a Plant who was a good example of the type. Expressed in everyday language this meant that a successful *company* needed one very creative and clever member. Creativity could be treated as an entity in itself and distinct from high intelligence and analytical ability (which might be termed cleverness). In this sense creativity in a Plant was more important than cleverness. But if both were combined at a high level in a single person this was a great advantage.

Creativity and cleverness, however, both had abrupt lower thresholds. For example a clever and very creative Plant could be a great asset to a *company* whereas a very creative Plant of only average cleverness was unlikely to make the grade, usually by failing to establish any team-role credibility in a *company*. The failure of a Plant to fulfil himself in his team-role was the most distinguishing mark of "winning" *companies* that were in fact non-winners. Plants that disappointed were sometimes found to be creative in an inappropriate way; for example they were literate rather than numerate or had little interest in the undertaking.

3. *A Fair Spread in Mental Abilities*

The spread in measured mental abilities appeared to have a material bearing on *company* fortunes. The best results were associated with *companies* containing one very clever Plant, another clever member, and a Chairman who had slightly higher than average mental ability while other members of the *company* were slightly *below* average in mental ability.

This formula is certainly not one at which we might have arrived by chance experience or by commonsense. Yet with hindsight some of the advantages of this pattern are easily seen. A brilliantly clever and creative Plant is an asset to a *company,* but only if ultimate responsibility lies with another (the Chairman). A visionary also needs the stimulus of another lively mind of similar calibre on whom he can sharpen his wits. Every group needs someone able to find the flaw in imaginatively conceived but possibly unsound propositions (the Monitor-Evaluator with his dry and intellectually dispassionate attributes). In the absence of a Monitor-Evaluator, another member of the group of the requisite mental ability could profitably interact with the Plant, except for another Plant who usually introduces specific team-role competition.

The positive advantage of having other team members of slightly lower mental ability had puzzled us for a while. A possible explanation was that the gap between them and their fellow members caused them to look for other positive team-roles: strong competition on one front had the effect of encouraging them to find ways of fulfilling themselves on other fronts. At any rate teams with a wide spread of scores in mental ability were observed to pull together better than teams that were intellectually more homogeneous.

4. *A Spread in Personal Attributes Offering Wide Team-Role Coverage*

Winning teams were also characterized by a membership which offered, on the evidence of their test scores, a good spread in likely team-roles. In the EME, winning teams seemed to need in particular one Completer and at least one Company Worker. For our own Teamopoly exercise which gave greater scope for negotiation, the Resource Investigator type of member figured prominently in winning teams. In both exercises there seemed advantages in having one good example of an introvert and another of an extrovert. Although there were differences in pay-off behaviour between the EME and Teamopoly, if a general point is to be made it is that a winning *company* has a wider range of team-role strengths on which to draw than less successful *companies*. Different types of member increase the range of a team while also minimising the unconstructive friction that occurs when two or more people compete for the same role.

5. *A Good Match between the Attributes of Members and their Responsibilities in the Team*

One mark of winning teams was the way in which members found useful jobs and team-roles that fitted their personal characteristics and abilities. It was impossible to forecast how this would work out, but retrospective analysis of records suggested it as a feature of winning teams.

In general it does not seem the rule that people get the work they deserve. It is more common to find that individuals take on jobs most in line with their experience irrespective of how well they have performed. In the less successful teams the allocation of work was dominated without any further thought by the claim to have done something like it in the past.

Winning teams on the other hand found ways of reducing their reliance and dependence on one individual for a critical function unless he had already shown signs of excelling. The way in which finance was sometimes handled illustrates the point. Many *companies* placed responsibility for finance into the hands of a Finance Director, usually the person who claimed to have had most financial experience. In a number of winning *companies* the risk of getting the wrong person in the job was minimized by a more flexible arrangement. For example, pairs of people would look after specific functions, one of which would be finance. A sharp-minded member could therefore work alongside someone used to dealing with figures. The flexible pairing system also provided an opportunity for an able member to transfer his attention to some other critical aspect of the *company's* activity, provided he showed the inclination and had a useful line. In other words the best match between people and jobs came about through allowing informal arrangement to modify any mismatches that would otherwise have existed.

6. *An Adjustment to the Realization of Imbalance*

Weaknesses can be compensated for by self-knowledge. While this is an accepted maxim governing individual behaviour its truth can be extended to groups. This sixth feature of winning teams came to the fore in Teamopoly. If it was less evident in our study of EME winners the reasons are understandable. During the early stage of the EME the participants were either not aware of or had only a fleeting acquaintance with the team-role theory of groups. It is rather doubtful whether even partial knowledge did much to help their team effectiveness. In some instances it made inter-personal adjustment within a team more difficult. For example, some members who fancied themselves as Plants played their team-roles in an overbearing and damaging way. They failed to take account of other team-roles of which they had less appreciation and which could be critical at certain stages in *company* affairs. In fact most of the real learning took place at the end of the exercise with the assistance of the debriefing, too late, of course, to influence personal behaviour.

In Teamopoly a very different situation prevailed. The seminar participants had already absorbed a fair amount of team-role theory and technique, and had engaged in some practical reinforcing exercises before Teamopoly began. This experience did not, however, always result in adaptive behaviour. Once Teamopoly started the excitement of the occasion caused many to forget what they had learned. There was difficulty in appreciating how a general theory could be applied in practice. But there were some teams in which members consciously took account of their potential team-role strengths, while being equally conscious of and compensating for their team-role weaknesses. These teams in making the most effective deployment of their resources could become runaway winners surprising themselves as much as others.

An example of a *company* which made an unusually good adjustment to the stark facts before it came from the most recent team-building seminar we ran in Cambridge. The team was entirely composed of Shapers. To add to the disadvantage with which this unbalanced *company* was burdened, only one member had performed well in the measure of mental ability. In this respect the Shaper *company* compared unfavourably with the other three *companies* against which it was competing. Once the team design had been published, the seminar participants were asked to make forecasts on the likely outcome of the exercise. The Shaper *company* was estimated as likely to finish last with the individual forecasts of the Shaper *company* members themselves according with the general verdict. When the Shaper *company* met for the first time its members took a doleful view of their collective prospects. In the event however the Shaper *company* not only won but won handsomely.

What happened was explained frankly and unequivocally in the debriefing report by the Shaper spokesman. "We realized that we had little chance of winning but we were determined to prove everyone wrong. Only one person had done well on the CTA. We concluded that as none of us had any brains we might as well make him the Plant. 'Go away and think up some ideas,' we said. Then we remembered what we had been told about a good Plant/Chairman alliance making for success. We reckoned that any one of us, being pretty managerial, could have acted as Chairman. We put it to our Plant:'You choose the Chairman you would like to work with.' From that moment things began to work well . . . But we couldn't stand having a Plant around for too long. So we made him the board player. When he came back from board play he had added insights on which to work. While he was away we realized that we had to make the best use of our time. Being Shapers we knew we were likely to argue a lot. So we decided to take a vote on every issue. That enabled us to make quick decisions and seize opportunities. We progressively acquired an attractive portfolio of properties. From then on it was plain sailing."

The value of seeing the important tasks in terms of the underlying team-roles was well illustrated by several other teams unbalanced in composition but with a good deal of self-insight. The prevailing pattern was that at its first meeting the team would identify its area of weakness and then appoint someone to look after the jobs that looked as though they belonged naturally to the missing team-role. For example, a team would discover that they lacked a Completer. The implication was that deadlines and schedules would be forgotten. One member of the team would therefore be appointed to cover this aspect of the team's operation, usually the member regarded as having personal characteristics closest to the missing team-role. The effect would be that the likely weakness of the team would not be exposed during the exercise, while the team would still succeed in playing to its strength. In other instances the discovery that a *company* had no Plant led to a search for the nearest team-role. This was usually that of the Resource Investigator, who was likely to be the most enterprising, or the Monitor-Evaluator, who was reckoned to be at least clever. One of these two would then set about creating some new ideas and strategies appropriate to the challenge ahead. This often worked out not too badly. As the team would have other strengths, the overall performance of the *company* would be a good deal higher than might have been guessed at the outset.

To summarize about winning teams, their main feature was their strength in those personal qualities and abilities associated with the key team-roles, together with a diversity of talent and personality making up the rest of the team. There was always someone suitable for any job that came up. Even teams with something less than the ideal distribution of talents could compensate for shortcomings by recognizing a latent weakness and deciding to do something about it.

WINNING TEAMS IN INDUSTRY

In due course it became plain that enough was known about winning management teams to transfer some of this experience to the industrial world. A company could learn whether its management team had any obvious deficiencies. If so it could take account of any shortcomings in recruiting to the management or even without changing its composition it could do much to improve the way in which it used its own resources. Two examples are here worth quoting.

> Hilltown Engineering Ltd was the largest employer of labour in a rural town in the West Country. In spite of its good industrial relations and generally happy atmosphere the firm's trading position had deteriorated until the holding company that owned it considered that something would have to be done. If no action was taken there was every likelihood that the firm would either have to be sold to a competitor or simply closed down. Another possible line of action was to install another manager in a rescue bid and that was the line eventually chosen. Since the firm was closely tied to the motor industry and difficult times were foreseen, the manager designate needed to be a person of more than average drive and mental acumen, hard and tough yet at the same time someone who could retain the good industrial relations that had been built up over the years.
> years.
>   After many well qualified candidates had presented themselves for the job, the eventual choice fell on John Bright, a manager in the Chairman/Shaper mould who had scored very highly in the measures of mental ability. As part of his apprenticeship John Bright attended our three-day team management seminar. The experience led to an in-company course, which while serving an educational role also helped

to pinpoint some of the imbalances in the management team of Hilltown Engineering. This information was shared amongst the executives and also helped Bright to assess the new team which he was to inherit. As a result a number of changes were made in general organization and in the allocation of responsibilities and duties, although in person and number the management team remained much the same.

John Bright now set up a number of management project teams to examine all the various problems the firm faced. In the year in which he took over, the company was still making a profit but had been budgeted to lose £600,000 in the following year. To add to this poor outlook a slump in the motor industry suddenly hit Hilltown Engineering. The company's best-selling product, manufactured under licence, was also threatened when the overseas company holding the licence announced that it was to be phased out.

To meet the gathering storm clouds Hilltown Engineering moved fast. In Bright's second year the firm's complement was reduced from 1,136 to 580 in an exercise that was remarkable for its smoothness; and the expected loss turned into a small profit. During this period a number of new ventures were started up. By the time of Bright's third year of office the company had been hit by the international oil crisis and their best-selling product had been completely withdrawn. Nevertheless on a complement now reduced to 530 people the company achieved a higher turnover than three years earlier when the work force had been more than twice as high. The net effect was a profit giving a 24% return on capital and in the following year, in spite of the unfavourable state of the market, a return of 21%.

The holding company now decided to promote Bright into a new job elsewhere. Unfortunately the effort that had gone into creating the team when Bright joined was not matched in recreating it after he left. Two years later the losses incurred were equivalent to an 11% loss on the capital employed and a year later this rose to a disastrous 43%.

Hilltown Engineering provides an example of how a single admission to a management team can change the fortunes of a company, initially in this case in a favourable direction. It also illustrates the rider; that a single subtraction from the team can have an equally momentous effect in the other direction unless the balance is re-established. Hence some firms have winning teams only at certain periods of their life history. Others find a formula for maintaining their winning streak and do so through their culture reinforced, and perhaps even promoted in the first place, by the way in which their personnel policies operate.

Turning round a company that is failing is a more difficult operation than enabling an up-and-coming company to maintain its momentum and progress and avoid falling into those pitfalls which analysis of its management team composition might suggest as likely. An able management team can sense its own faults and do something about them. An example is Simpson Ltd, based in Adelaide, which became interested and involved in our team-building activities during my first Australian tour. By the time I returned two years later I was surprised to find the good use to which the firm had put the knowledge it had gained. On this second visit all the senior executives took the tests. This enabled us to learn something further about the management team that ran Simpson and also provided a basis for seeing how the teams that we arranged for purposes of training performed in the Teamopoly exercise.

The Simpson group operates in the home appliance "whitegoods" industry, being best known in Australia for its washing machines, clothes dryers, and cookers. A progressive reduction of tariffs in Australia's hitherto highly protected market and too many producers operating in the home market had been amongst the problems which put the firm into the red. Eventually a new chief executive was appointed who set about the task of pulling the company round. The first step was to make a number of changes amongst the top executive appointments which inevitably had an unsettling effect on the others. This disturbance was but temporary. Those executives whose services were to be retained in the key positions were assured that the company still wanted them. The vacancies that had been created were gradually filled with hand-picked young men of high ability. The backlog of mistrust and suspicion was gradually overcome by an emphasis on open management. Team working became the order of the day and the uniting force that linked older established members of the company with the new faces that had been promoted or introduced. Each product business was now run by a multi-disciplinary management team. The experience not only had a maturing effect on the groups themselves but also on personal development. Individuals were spotted and judged as being suitable for joining other teams where their abilities could be better utilized.

After the various changes had been completed test results on the top management team showed a very good approximation to the classic mixed team pattern. The team-roles of Chairman, Plant, Team Worker, Resource Investigator, Monitor-Evaluator and Company Worker were all well covered. The effect of recruiting executives of high ability had, however, showed some signs of creating dangers of an Apollo syndrome elsewhere in the organization. A high level of scores on mental ability was recorded, the highest of any company we had tested. Since some of the youngest managers recruited spent most of their time running their own sections this had not so far created any obvious problems. But less impressive was the state of teamwork at this level. In our Teamopoly exercise we decided therefore to set up a typical Apollo team. In spite of all the previous training in teamwork that Simpson had given, the Apollo team ran into the expected difficulties. Its members worked out and acted on their own approaches; conflicts were left unresolved and there was little coordination. The Apollo team finished poorly, a result which the other Simpson teams received with some amusement and a certain lack of sympathy.

Simpson's approach to management has enabled the firm to make continuous progress so that it is now one of Australia's most flourishing manufacturing companies. Over a period of five years the group volume of turnover has increased four times in markets which themselves had shown little growth in total. Market share of the individual product businesses has moved progressively from an average of 20%–30% to an average of 55%–85%. Profitability has increased by an average of 25% each year and the company's share prices have quadrupled. The company is rapidly increasing its rate of investment and new overseas operations have been or are in the process of being set up.

The seminars we conducted were much influenced by the concept of the classic mixed team and were about how that balance could be best adjusted either by recruitment of a suitable person to fill a gap or by team-role adjustment within the team. This approach was governed by the fact that the classic mixed team had proved the most reliable of winning teams in our studies. A further consideration was that the concept was unfamiliar so that firms felt that there was something new to be learned. In fact it was very difficult to point to a firm that was already actively employing this concept.

OTHER SUCCESSFUL PATTERNS

The classic mixed team was not however the only type of winning team. Other patterns figured amongst the winners, less complex in character and more commonly encountered in industry than the classic mixed team.

The best runner-up in the results league was the team of co-operative stable extroverts. This type of team only occasionally won, but it frequently came second and seldom did badly. Its members did not contain any great spread of team types, being mainly Team Workers and Resource Investigators with Company Workers as a secondary team-role. Provided the team was well equipped with a reasonably good level of mental ability, they did not seem to suffer from lack of a Monitor Evaluator or Plant. In fact the clear distinctions in team-role in this type of *company* were less evident than usual. What they had missed in specialized behaviour they made up for in flexibility. "All the world's a stage and one man in his time plays many parts"; and it was difficult at times to know who was playing which part. All the actors were heavily engaged. As people they loved working in teams, enjoyed each other's company, talked a great deal and discussed everything together. But the pattern was not as chaotic as it might seem to the casual onlooker. Animated interaction led to collectively produced ideas which seemed beyond their individual reach.

If there was one weakness to which this team was subject it was complacency and euphoria to which stable extroverts tend in general to be prone. Eventually we were able to improve the design by introducing another extrovert of a somewhat different type, a Shaper. One Shaper adequately served a team of easy-going extroverts ensuring that there was someone around to crack the whip whenever a discrepancy opened up between objective reality and a team's optimistic estimates of its own position.

Moving down the results league two other types of winning team were found. Yet neither could commend themselves as patterns which others might follow. The reservation about both these team types is that their failures were no less conspicuous than their successes.

The first of these occasionally very successful teams was one in which the leadership was firmly in the hands of a superstar. More concretely this was a team in which the Chairman would have unrivalled superiority in intellectual or creative ability over his colleagues. His office and his natural talents reinforced each other in establishing his ascendency. This allowed the *company* to operate a coherent strategy, to use flair to advantage, and to make a quick decision when the occasion demanded. Morale amongst the team members would even stand up well provided the *company* was achieving results. Lack of opposition to the superstar Chairman made for streamlined operation. With the right formula such a *company* could achieve good results but if there was anything wrong it would be slow to take corrective action. The dominant leader could provide an overall grasp that would enable a team to move forward unwaveringly to its objective but equally he might lead his flock up some blind alley and none would think of turning back until the point of crisis had already been reached. Superstar-led teams had a way of hastening either to the top of the results table or to the bottom.

The final winning team that merits attention is the Apollo *company*. This has been fully discussed in Chapter Two. The Apollo *company* is one which hoards mental ability so that it has ample resources and talents for dealing with the most complex problems but suffers from extreme difficulty in being able to use what it has. In general Apollo *companies* performed poorly but they did occasionally win. Under the right Chairman and with the right culture sufficiently good, or adequate, teamwork could be established to enable their assets to be realized.

To take stock, several types of team have figured amongst the winners. The first is the classic mixed team where team-roles tend to be well differentiated; by track record the most successful of all teams. The second is what might be called the typical participative group, comprising stable extroverts with a liking for group work and whose team-roles tend to be undifferentiated. And the final two types are teams which either are led by or consist mainly of talented and clever people.

How far do these teams which have emerged as the most consistently effective over the years in our experimental studies compare with the teams that run the most successful companies in the business world? Do the same underlying principles and patterns apply, or do they not?

Answers to these questions are not easy to provide. Certainly successful companies can be identified by their record of performance: the main difficulty lies in finding an adequate means of describing how these companies are run and who runs them.

Nevertheless some useful insights can be gained by looking closely at a few very successful companies which have features relevant to the theme of our inquiry.

TEAM PRACTICE IN THREE COMPANIES

The United Kingdom has had a less than distinguished post-war industrial record. If we omit multinationals and confine ourselves to indigenous companies that have been consistently successful, we end up with a small field. From this group I have picked three, one each to represent distribution, industry and services: Marks & Spencer, ICI, and the BBC. Marks & Spencer must be one of Britain's most successful retail stores, famed for its quality of product, its standard of service, the treatment of its staff, and its record of profitability. ICI has been chosen as one of Britain's biggest and most successful industries, a model employer, where high-level expanding technology and commercial success go hand in hand. The BBC commends itself on different grounds. It is a public corporation and not therefore subject to the normal commercial criteria. Its strength lies in its reputation. It has been hailed as Britain's best ambassador and its most successful TV productions have made their mark around the world. One particular reason for choosing the BBC is that the success or failure of its TV production teams can in a sense be measured. Some programmes are so unsuccessful that they never see the light of day. Others attract a large viewing public and create their own export market.

Common Features

Before we consider these companies separately we may note what they have in common. All three companies are heavy recruiters of University graduates. ICI annually recruits more qualified scientists than any other firm in the UK. The BBC recruits graduates not only for critical jobs, such as script writers but also for a wide range of jobs that are intellectually undemanding. In the case of Marks & Spencer about half of all assistant store managers are graduates, a figure unparalleled in the UK retail trade. Since all three organizations fill their senior positions almost entirely through internal promotion it is clear that their personnel policy offers as candidates for the management team a steady supply of well-educated young men and women of good mental ability with in-depth experience of the industry.

Marks & Spencer has centrally located shops in almost every town of any size in the UK but, apart from a computer installation, the whole Marks & Spencer organization is in fact housed in its Head Office in Baker Street, London. Such centralization could make the company very susceptible to rigidity, especially as it has a well-defined management structure. This danger is offset by the importance given to the operation of its management teams and its communication groups.

The Board of Marks & Spencer consists of twenty-two directors. In practice most top management decision-making stems from the regular meetings of the Chairman's Advisory Committee. This management executive group consists of the Chairman and four regular members plus the occasional specialist who will be invited in as a resource from time to time. Every month the Chairman will hold information meetings which up to eighty senior people will attend. Departmental managers will hold their own information meetings for between ten and twenty people. At the level of the store, communication groups regularly meet. They usually comprise twelve or thirteen people with each area of the store represented. Employees can raise any points they wish at these meetings, while at the same time they are told about all that is going on.

On the operational side, teams meet regularly at the Marks & Spencer Head Office to discuss any major plans and changes that relate to their area of the business. These meetings are easy to arrange since all the key people connected with any given section of the business are likely to be found on one floor of each block of offices that surround a courtyard. A feature of these business meetings is that, while the meeting is kept fairly small, several levels of the hierarchy are usually represented. The rather larger Merchandising Review made up of twenty people might contain members from seven levels – the Director of the merchandising group, a senior executive, an executive, a merchandising manager, the merchandiser, a selector and a technologist. At these meetings the senior people are there as of right but those at junior levels have to be nominated by those above them. In this way some form of control is exercised over the composition of the meeting and juniors get an early chance to shine.

In addition to these regular meetings informal meetings are frequent as part of a general policy of close co-ordination and as a means of ensuring that important points of detail receive close attention and are looked at from all possible angles. By the time a new member joins the top management team he will often already have become highly experienced as a team man. The social basis of management softens the effect of centralization thereby reducing the risk that the demise or retirement of any one key manager would produce an upheaval liable to undermine the viability and prosperity of any one business section or of the company as a whole.

Marks & Spencer and ICI are both examples of *winning* companies in their own separate fields. Both companies are highly participative and consultative in their social, business, and industrial relationships. But while Marks & Spencer is highly centralized, ICI places an emphasis on decentralization except on certain overriding issues.

ICI is organized into ten major divisions and also runs nine subsidiary companies. Each division prides itself on its distinctive culture and values its autonomy. The way in which centralization and decentralization work together is well illustrated in relation to graduate recruitment. Like other large companies, ICI operates on the "milk round" of British Universities. The initial exercise is undertaken by CURV (the Co-ordinated University Recruitment Venture). The "milkroundsmen" drawn from different divisions give initial interviews at the various universities to about half of those who complete application forms. A list goes to ICI Head Office which then circulates the divisions on short-listed candidates. That is where CURV ends. The divisions then adopt their own preferred selection procedures. Some divisions employ a comprehensive battery of selection tests to aid them in the selection process. Other divisions do not use tests at all. Divisions that use tests do not necessarily employ the same test battery. Within a division there may even be differences of practice: for example, mechanical engineers will be carefully screened with the aid of selection tests, while chemical engineers are not, the difference being accounted for merely by the differing viewpoints of the managers in these sections. However there are common rules that apply: all appointees are offered specific jobs within the section of those who interview them and divisions are not allowed to "top" an offer when they are competing for the same candidate.

In spite of certain differences in recruitment practice there are two factors which, taken together, have given a certain distinctiveness to ICI as a company over the years. The first factor is that great emphasis is placed on the academic calibre of those recruited. Only graduates with good degrees are considered, while there is also a tendency, rare in industry, to recruit those with research doctorates. There was even a time when PhD chemists were recruited to run chemical plants in the belief that this was the best way of getting hold of a high-calibre managerial elite. In due course other methods were found to yield more satisfactory results. Over the years methods may have changed but the aim of recruiting the "best" has remained constant. The second common factor of note is the emphasis placed on group training once graduates are recruited. The clever young graduate is socialized almost as soon as he enters the company not only by industrial training methods but by immersion in the culture of ICI. One academic study by a sociologist likened the company to a club. The club atmosphere acts as a powerful counter to the recruitment tendency that would otherwise turn ICI into an Apollo company.

The third UK *winning* company differs from our first two by being much less concerned with participation, consultation, and group working generally. The BBC as an employer is referred to by many of its employees, as well as by outsiders, as Auntie. A certain avuncular patronage (or its feminine equivalent!) is part of its heritage. Yet arts graduates as well as engineering apprentices are strongly attracted to employment in the BBC. This gives the BBC the opportunity to take its pick of talented applicants, but creates a problem later on as to how they can best be absorbed into effective working groups.

All television programmes are created by relatively small teams. In practice, teams are continuously forming and reforming. Every programme is a one-off event. Such a background makes it difficult to formulate a coherent and consistent personnel policy. People join programmes as they become available and by invitation. The team formation process operates in a mysterious way: line management has a hand in it; a crucial influence is also exercised by those who have a major part to play in the programme. Key people feel the need for a greater say. Film directors, authors, script writers, star actors, camera men, and cutting editors may all acquire reputations as distinguished professionals. Creative artists aspire to run programmes that give full scope to their own creative individuality; yet they all want to work with those who are at the top of their own professional tree. These two aspirations are not easily combined.

What is recognized by those with responsibilities in the area is that the BBC is in effect laden with Plants. Plants are often unreasonable about who they are prepared to work with and the terms under which they are prepared to operate. But they are also capable of behaving in uncharacteristic ways. What is observed is that one Plant may be such a star that other lesser Plants will be prepared to work with him by giving way on more points than usual in the cause of professional fulfilment. Since this whole process involves a most complex pattern of human relationships and is somewhat unpredictable, management does not always intervene directly by insisting that particular individuals join particular teams. Recognizing that people can work with some crew members but not with others, management offers some latitude to the most talented performers, allowing them scope for creating their own teams. Other teams come together by mutual arrangement. This policy has to be reconciled with a basic strategy of using available resources as fully and economically as possible. A certain amount of positive allocation of people is therefore necessary. There are a number of Shaper/Plants who seem capable of putting into operation their own programmes but otherwise management has to engage in a delicate balancing operation in forming its production teams. By so doing it assures the production of a limited number of television programmes of outstanding merit while also allowing the general output target of programmes to be maintained.

TEAM-ROLE THEORY AND WINNING COMPANIES

If we relate these three enterprises to the conclusions we reached about winning teams under experimental conditions, we may see that each has found its own mainstream solution to the management team problem. In effect Marks & Spencer has developed a pattern that is in line with stable extrovert teams and this is broadly confirmed by what they appear to look for in selecting candidates. Plants are not needed in these teams, but a good general level of mental ability is assured by the nature of the recruitment process. Team members *prove* themselves in junior teams, and as they move between one team and another generate material evidence in terms of which their suitability for promotion can be judged. Once Marks & Spencer had become a thriving company with sound policies that had stood the test of time, the problem of how to get a good management team largely resolved itself by a tradition that had been built up. Here it is fair to talk about the establishment of a Marks & Spencer culture.

In cultural terms there are in fact affinities between Marks & Spencer and ICI: the emphasis on care of the employee; the importance given to high standards; and belief in participation, consultation, and team working. But ICI requires its own distinctive "solution" to the problem of recruiting the management teams which run its divisions. On the one hand it has the image of an establishment company–a headmaster once likened it to the Bank of England – but on the other, the prosperity of the company depends on continuous progress in pushing back the frontiers of science in a chemical and industrial setting against an international rather than just a domestic background. ICI therefore requires its share of clever pioneering people if its rate of progress is to be maintained. The academic standards laid down for its entrants and its rigorous selection procedures ensure that it has an abundance of talent even at the risk of an overkill. The dilemma here is that the company is caught between serving its cultural and business aims. This danger is offset to some extent by the emphasis given to training the able graduates the company recruits in group work. The effect, then, is that the company is recruiting potential Apollo members whose individual talents are needed for the difficult tasks ahead, but is striving to ensure that it does not end up with typical Apollo groups.

The BBC, for its part, may be compared with ICI for the high standard it demands of its intake, though more specifically it seeks Plants. Like ICI, it risks an overkill to guarantee that it acquires the talent it demands. Apollo teams occur frequently and are recognized for what they are. They are often chaotic in style and atmosphere. But the experiences generated at least allow for the emergence, through survival of the fittest, of the superstar-led team. This is one of our four types of winning company; not a reliable one, but one which is capable at times of reaching the heights of achievement.

If there are any general features that govern successful companies in the business world, one may be that they have learned to devise ways of operating like co-operative stable extrovert teams without actually recruiting stable extroverts. Winning companies are keen to ensure that they recruit candidates with high initial ability: they rely to some extent on the culture to ensure that those selected end up as proficient in team working.

The most successful team in our experimental studies – the classic mixed team – does not seem as yet to figure amongst winning teams in the business world. Why is this? It may be that such teams do exist but are very difficult to detect. Even so we might have expected to see more traces of them. Their scarcity, if real, may be explained on several counts. Firstly, the concept is not easily grasped especially if the underlying complexities are to be understood; secondly, there is a natural human resistance to searching for the mixed team as a deliberate act of policy, for like selects like and people usually create groups in their own image; thirdly, good material for mixed teams may be suspect in the eyes of company selectors who are often searching for the ideal rounded man. But as Shakespeare reminds us in *Measure for Measure*:

> They say best men are moulded out of faults and, for the most, become much more the better for being a little bad.

In the mixed teams there is always someone present to underpin a weakness and who will be fulfilled by so doing. Such a brief calls not only for good team working but also for both modesty and sophistication.

CONCLUSIONS

What then are the implications of this chapter? In practice the classic mixed team provides the most consistently good results. But to put such a team together must be an intricate operation demanding high skills from the selector. Any disturbance of the team can easily upset the balance. This is why there is much to be said for forming a group whose members are less specialized in their functions and abilities. Team-orientated stable extroverts, well disciplined and of reasonably good mental ability, produce consistently good teams, covering between themselves all the various functions that have to be performed. Such teams have the advantage that their members can be combined and recombined in other teams without much loss of efficiency. The firm that is committed to a consultative, participative style of management and seeks versatile, general utility managers, can look for candidates that are typical members of our second type of winning team. For very large companies this policy has much to commend it. The alternative option of moving towards the classic model of winning teams could be a formidable task. Large organizations are likely to experience difficulty in exercising control over the composition of their senior management teams since so many forces impinge upon the politics of promotion. Here small companies are at an advantage.

Our two other types of winning team are both capable of achieving great things though liable to founder.

The superstar-led team, where one highly talented or creative individual dominates his colleagues and leads "from the front", has limited scope in large enterprises under prevailing social and economic conditions. It has to be remembered, however, that this pattern has met with considerable success in the past. If authoritarianism is to survive as a competitive system this is a formula to give it life. In small firms the superstar-led team may still produce good results for a long time to come. Nonetheless it cannot be confidently recommended in any general way. Over-dependence on a single individual is a prescription for everlasting uncertainty over what the future offers.

The problem of over-dependence on a single individual is overcome when we look at the Apollo team, the type of team that we may expect to find running high technology firms. Here the need to recruit well-qualified and able young men who can operate on the frontiers of technology predetermines the type of management that will emerge under these conditions. There are prospects that a few of these Apollo-run firms will prosper. A good Apollo Chairman or a rapid turnover of young Apollo managers allowing only the fittest to survive will increase the chances of success.

Winning companies vary in the character of the teams that manage them: yet after years of experiments in composing teams and encouraging others to try out their own designs and after much searching after successful examples in the industrial world, we must conclude that the choice in proven patterns remains strictly limited.

9:   Ideal Team Size

How many people should we have in a team? To some extent the answer must depend on the amount of work that needs to be performed. But the notion of an ideal number is worth pursuing where members of a management team spend their time deliberating together. Before we look at the leads which our experiments can offer, a few points of a general nature are worth making about the effect of group size on behaviour.

GROUPS AND INDIVIDUAL BEHAVIOUR

In general it seems that the bigger the group the greater are the unseen pressures that make for conformity. These pressures may become so cogent in mass meetings, congregations and assemblies that an appearance – or illusion – of unanimity is created.

Behaviour within the group is further complicated by group structure. The stronger the structure, the less tolerance there is for dissenters or for any form of deviant expression. Where groups are unstructured – that is to say large numbers of people meet for a purpose but without any imposed constraints – the individual, rather than recovering a sense of mature individuality, is apt to revel in the anonymity which size offers. A crowd freed from social control becomes a mob. One way or another large gatherings of people exercise such an influence over their constituents that each person becomes either excessively passive, or, if full self-expression is permitted, inclined to irresponsible behaviour, aggressive verbal declarations, or even acts of destruction.

Why should the individual lose his sense of mature identity and ability to contribute in a positive way in large groups? Part of the answer may be that sheer numbers force him to play a non-role so that for the time being, at least, his personality is diminished. Consider, say, a meeting of a hundred people conducted along democratic lines with all members invited to contribute from the floor. Let us imagine that the Chairman wished every person to contribute equally and that he allotted time accordingly. Then for an hour each person would talk for one per cent and listen for ninety-nine per cent of the time. With perfect regulation each speaker would have thirty-six seconds. This would make it impossible for anyone to say anything useful.

TEAMS OF TEN MEMBERS

Now suppose we reduce the number in the meeting by a factor of ten. Suppose again that conversation is shared equally, with people talking in turn rather than simultaneously. Then each person will be talking ten per cent of the time and listening ninety per cent. While this arrangement sounds far more workable, it still means that everyone will be cast in a mainly passive role. What makes the arrangement less feasible still is that in a peer group individuals vary appreciably in their talkativeness. A dominant person will be disinclined to restrain himself for ninety per cent of the time, while a recessive individual whose fair ration, as it were, is ten per cent of the talking time is more likely to say nothing at all. If a group contains several dominant people the competition for talking space can lead to continuous interruptions or simultaneous monologues. This outcome seldom satisfies anyone.

While a unit size of ten looks too large for a group of peers conferring in a team, it is a different matter once a group becomes formalized. The strength of a structure, one is aware, depends on the nature of the cells which make it up and on their arrangement. Here there are lessons to be learned from the past. History must grant the Roman army the honour of being the longest surviving organization based on power that the world has ever known. That army was arranged in multiple tiers with the person in charge at each level having ten people reporting directly to him. A commander who addresses ten people can do so without raising his voice and he can count on his fingers to ensure they are all present. He can talk for most of the time, issuing instructions and directions, and there should still be time available for anyone to raise any queries or relevant observations. For a streamlined chain of command ten looks the ideal number as the base unit for organization. Perhaps it is no coincidence that the army of the Incas, the most enduring ancient civilization of the Americas, had a similar unit size and arrangement.

The syndicates at the Administrative Staff College, Henley, consisted of ten or eleven members – with a measure of authority being invested in an appointee – in this case a Chairman. Management education may not have been around as long as the Roman army but at least it can be said that this size of syndicate has proved itself since the College syndicate working began. The Chairman in controlling proceedings would draw on the resources of the group to enable a wide variety of views to be brought to bear on the subject or problem under review. By creating a need for listening, the essentially educational nature of the activity reduced the level of active participation to the point where ten or eleven became a most suitable number. This group size offered advantages too for those periodic recreations which served to cement the personal bonds between syndicate members. Ten could fit into two cars.

Ten or eleven seemed to be a number that was large enough to give adequate variety in the possible range of social permutations that can enrich life but small enough to allow the syndicate to retain a sense of intimate group identity. It seems no coincidence that outside the village pub, to which the syndicate members were wont to retire, we find the village green on which eleven villagers play cricket during the summer; and in the field behind the pub we find the football pitch on which another team represent the village during the winter – again with eleven members. Can ten or eleven be the ideal size of structured human groups involving close personal relationships? If so, some might see in this an echo of the primeval male hunting band designed to use its strength and wits to advantage in the pursuit of large game. The quarry may have changed but the game remains, with an etymological consistency of Freudian character. The essentials of the team are retained too. The main difference is one of outward form as the carnivores sublimate themselves in team sport.

MEDIUM-SIZED TEAMS

The advantage of a unit of ten or eleven members seems to recede when a team of this size meets around a table to thrash out plans and policies with a view to making decisions. There is scarcely enough scope for everyone to engage in a fair share of talking without unduly prolonging the decision-making business or reducing its efficiency. To disengage would also cause problems. It would be impolite to read a newspaper. Everyone has to look interested and attend. Nor does the purpose of the occasion provide the educational stimulus that the typical Henley syndicate enjoys and which in a sense occupies the unoccupied.

In an empirical way, and without any intervention on the part of the experimenters, Henley had come to the conclusion at an early stage that, for the purpose of playing a business game, a *company* of ten or eleven members was too large. A reduction was made to eight members. In time even this proved on the big side. In practice an EME *company* tended to be dominated by two, three or four prime movers, there would be one or two others marginally occupied and the remainder contributed little and became bored and dissatisfied. The College then reduced the number to six. The six-man *company* was found to be a more stable and enduring group and the greater part of our experiments were therefore conducted in teams of this size. That then raised the more general question of whether there is an optimum size for a team meeting round a table.

At this point an obvious objection suggests itself. As we have previously identified eight complementary team-roles and found the characteristics of individuals who best fit them, is there not a case for forming an ideal team of eight members? And, if so, why in the event should a team of six have proved more satisfactory?

The team of eight holds out promise but arouses misgivings. Its size is intermediate between, on the one hand, the ideal command group, and on the other hand, a small intimate circle who can act and talk together in concert at a mutually acceptable level of contribution and involvement without needing to interrupt each other.

Now it could be argued that a team of eight can reach its potential only if it is highly structured with a suitable person as Chairman and with its members appropriately selected and briefed so that the eight team-roles are covered by a person well fitted to perform each one. That is a tall order. Even if eight people of the right type were assembled it might still be difficult to ensure that they developed those mutual expectations that would allow them to interrelate in the theoretically ideal way. In any case such an intricate arrangement is hardly necessary. We have already observed that most competent managers seem able to function well in both a primary and a secondary team-role. In other words we do not *need* eight managers to perform eight team-roles. By a doubling up of team-roles, four managers could cover all eight. On this model the minimum number needed to cover all team-roles would be four. That allows nothing for the overlap that is likely to occur between members in either their primary or secondary team-roles, nor does it allow any one person such as the Chairman or the Plant to concentrate on a single team-role.

SMALLER TEAMS

The number six therefore is a fair compromise figure, coming as it does between eight which, except as an ideal, is too big and four which, except as another type of ideal, is too small. Yet in practice a target *company* size of six was not always obtainable. Members of course do not always divide exactly by that number and it was not uncommon to have one or two *companies* of seven members. The seven-man *company* in terms of resources had a numerical advantage over the others. But this did not seem to be much of an asset. For some reason the seven-man *companies* did not perform so well as the six-man *companies*. It may be the former were just that bit too big to be efficient.

In the Henley management game (EME) the six-man *companies* portioned out their responsibilities along conventional lines. One person would be Chairman, a second would look after finance; a third, marketing; a fourth, production; a fifth, management services; and a sixth might combine purchasing with the job of acting as the Company Secretary.

This functional division of work allowed each member to establish his own work territory and avoided the conflict that overlapping responsibilities tend to engender. As most *companies* gave to their members those jobs which corresponded most closely with the work they normally performed, confidence was instilled through doing something that was familiar. Yet as the specific tasks that fell to each member of the *company* used up only a small proportion of their available time, the members had ample opportunity to play their parts in group discussion. It was this opportunity, derived from a degree of under-employment, that set the scene in which team-roles were to emerge. A team of six could offer a broad range of technical skills and team-roles so that a *company* could achieve, if its composition was favourable, a high degree of balance. This was valuable in itself as an educational experience. In general terms, it is not without significance that, for a period of at least a decade, six endured as the number that was found, on the internal evidence at Henley, to be most suitable for enabling a management team to tackle a complex problem.

When teams are involved in high rates of activity there is a danger that the larger or medium-sized team becomes inefficient since problems arise in co-ordinating its various parts. This was borne out in the case of Teamopoly – an exercise that made simultaneous demands on decision-making and action, and so created crises for a *company* in sorting out its priorities and dealing with conflicting urgencies. Greater pressure was exerted by giving each *company* four members instead of six as in the EME at Henley. In many instances, the four members were brought together precisely because they were not complementary. All this was part of our design strategy to bring to the fore the differences in the behaviour of teams composed along different lines and to relate their behaviour to their team-role composition. The four-man *company*, of whatever composition, could not cover all the vicissitudes and predicaments that came its way. Lack of time, though a source of difficulty, was not the prime problem. There were in fact periodic intervals during the exercise in which major strategic questions could have been sorted out. What is of interest is that every winning *company* in Teamopoly including those of more orthodox design made at least one major strategic mistake during the exercise. In the EME at Henley, on the other hand, there was less to criticize in the way that winning teams performed.

Under favourable circumstances, team balance was easier to achieve in the six-man *companies* of the EME than in the four-man *companies* of Teamopoly. If, in human resources, the four-man team tended to be less well equipped than a six-man team to tackle a complex problem, there were at least counterbalancing advantages. The four-man *company* achieved a level of intimacy, involvement and excitement that the six-man *company* could never quite match. This does not mean that the team was more integrated; rather that relations were more intense. Love, hate, humour, exuberance and exasperation abounded. One seminar member declared himself unable to say goodbye to a fellow team member for fear that tears would well up in his eyes. Yet another felt bound to register a complaint about a fellow team member. The four-man team engendered relationships not dissimilar to those that belong to a family where only a narrow margin separates the varied emotions that closeness brings. Just as all families are happy in the same way but unhappy families are unhappy in their own peculiar way; so also we might say of the four-man team: if they got on well they were harmonious and positive on all fronts; but where relationships did not work out the cross-currents seemed immensely complicated.

THE CHAIRMAN AND TEAM SIZE

One possible reason for the observed differences between teams of four and six revolves round chairmanship. With six in a team there was always someone in the chair. There was a certain cool formality about proceedings. On the other hand a team of four, though occasionally a Chairman might be elected, more often turned into a leaderless group. It became unstable at moments of crisis. It operated well only when complementary team-role relationships were established and depended on good team-role design from the outset.

If a Chairman is seen as one who holds the balance in a group then number plays a part in his emergence. In a team of four a Chairman in the case of conflict has two on one side and one on the other. No casting vote is required. The job seems hardly necessary. In a team of six the emerging Chairman would deal with two on the one hand and three on the other. Still no casting vote is called for; nevertheless, the greater team size suggests the need for someone to organize the resources of the group. Now take the intermediary team size of five. The case for a Chairman here is overwhelming. The group is large enough to benefit from organization, while the casting vote becomes decisive should uncertainty or disagreement threaten.

Five-man teams only occurred in our experiments in an unpre-meditated way. With a target team size of six the number was occasionally and unavoidably reduced to five either because there were insufficient course members to make every *company* up to six or because of the enforced absence of a member of a six-man *company* from illness or other causes. On one course at Henley there were two *companies* with five members and six with six members. The two five-member *companies* finished first and second. On another course three five-member *companies* finished fifth, seventh and eighth but in these instances the *companies* contained members who had not taken the tests–a sign associated for some reason with an unfavourable prognosis, (see Chapter Seven). There were other scattered five-member *companies* over the years but not in sufficient numbers to indicate any decisive advantage over teams comprising six members. What can be said is that five-man *companies* tended on the whole to be well-regulated *companies*. If they had the talent they made good use of what they had.

DANGERS OF TOO SMALL A TEAM

If a Chairman holds an easy balance in a five-man team, could he not do so with equal distinction in a three-man team? Is not a three-man team the shining example of a compact group offering the maximum in the way of involvement for its members?

It is interesting to speculate on how three-man teams might have fared pitted against those with four, five or six members. We have no real evidence as to what might have been achieved. What does seem apparent is that the "Chairman" of such a team would be something of a misnomer, if by the term Chairman we mean someone who is skilled in using the resources of the group. The Chairman of a three-man team would have more in common with a one-man team than with a Chairman of a five-man team. In other words he is close to being a boss with two subordinates.

Three men of high ability and complementary skills could become very effective if they act in unison. However the word team now becomes only marginally relevant. The point about a team is that it enjoys a life of its own. Its membership may change but it still continues. Its authority does not depend on or demand the presence of any single individual. The same cannot be said for a three-man team. Decisions are inextricably linked with personalities and if one person is absent business cannot continue without the risk of seriously changing the line that might otherwise have been taken.

A political example of a three-man team was demonstrated in Russia after the rejection of the "cult of personality". The favoured troika kept the Chairman of the Politburo, the Prime Minister, and the Party Secretary in harness. It formed a halfway house between a dictatorship and management by a full team, having some of the advantages of both. Other countries have produced their own troikas which in their particular versions make for a more streamlined and consistent form of management than a Prime Minister and a cabinet of between twelve and twenty ministers.

Industrial examples of troikas usually rest on the relationships established between the company Chairman (or in the U.S. the Corporation President), the Managing Director, and the (operational) General Manager. Often major decisions are taken by these three in the first place and later ratified by a management executive or the board. In both political and industrial cases an essential feature of the troika is that each of its members has responsibilities that span the whole field. Because a troika member is not responsible for a department or ministry he can concentrate on developing his team-role relationships with the other two members and is not impeded by limited responsibilities to push a particular set of interests that may run counter to what best serves the firm or the system as a whole.

Three members, as we have observed, may make for stable policy but they also make a team vulnerable. Even the smallest changes may affect its cohesion. Reducing bigness has the effect of magnifying the uncertainties that attach to particular personalities. As we proceed down the scale of team size we inevitably reach a crossover point where the team is no longer a team as such but an individual with supporters. When that happens any decisions that are taken tend to last only so long as that leading individual is around. Therein lies the weakness of autocrats, even benevolent autocrats. As soon as death intervenes or the throne becomes vacant for whatever cause, the empire or firm changes direction and character. The emphasis which dominated a leader's thinking for years becomes negated within a few months or even weeks.

If we are thinking about real life, rather than management games, then the trio, we may suggest, is the point at which the team runs up against the risk of being too small to withstand later challenge. If we are thinking about efficiency, then the composition of the trio leaves no margin for error.

From what has been said the ideal size of a team is a matter of compromise between conflicting forces. On the one hand there is a need to widen the composition, bringing in the full range of knowledge, experience and ability. The wishes of individuals or representatives to participate through consultation or the political desirability of securing commitment of all departments are amongst the many pressures that operate to inflate numbers. Yet on the other hand there is the need to reduce noise and maximize involvement and individual effectiveness by keeping the team small.

TEAM SIZE AND THE ENVIRONMENT

There are certain factors in the physical environment which can also have a bearing on ideal team size. This was brought home to us at Henley. The stately home which the College occupies contains rooms of unequal dimensions. Nor is the furniture standard; in particular the tables vary in size and shape, some being of moderate dimensions while others seem designed for conferences. A conference table in a room of moderate size had the effect of minimizing movement around the table. One member of a team would be less likely to go round to the other side to confer with another. Less use was made of visual aids and charts on free-standing boards. The shape of the table also had a bearing on the way in which the team operated. A Chairman sitting himself at the head of a long rectangular table was inclined to run his company in a strictly formal fashion, whereas those seated around a square or nearly square table acted like members of a peer group.

> Observations on the importance of table characteristics had struck one lady member of the College who after finishing the course secured an appointment with an oriental company that was setting up an office in London. At the first meeting Miss Shoesmith had noted that an uncomfortable atmosphere prevailed. She observed that the table was an unusually high one, especially for executives who were smaller than the average European. They clearly had difficulty in writing their reports. As soon as the executives had departed for their homeland Miss Shoesmith set about reducing the height of the table until she judged the top of it to be at an ideal distance from the ground. On the next trip to London the visiting executives were delighted to note the improvement, and a friendly accord developed amongst all attending the business conference.

Tables and rooms have an important bearing on the social organization of management. In spite of this many firms underestimate the need for meeting rooms and give little thought to their specification. The result is that there is usually nothing available between the standard office, which is too small, and one full conference room which is vast.

Teams expand so as to fill the rooms available to hold them. Teams then become ideal for the rooms but not for the purpose for which they are set up. Conversely teams shrink in membership to fit into available offices, thereby creating the impression, not unjustifiably, that major decisions are taken by small cliques.

If firms and institutions are to recognize the importance and potential of well-balanced teams, they must provide rooms and tables that are ideal for their use. It is better to build a room to suit the needs of the ideal team than to modify the composition of the team in the interests of fitting it into the room.

Tables

When a table comes to be designed or ordered much thought needs to be given to how many, ideally, will meet around it. Is the table to serve a command structure wherein managers will offer edicts and information to their underlings? Or is the intention that people will converse with each other freely and openly?

There are many implications attached to the design and size of conference tables. In the world of international politics the choice of conference table has sometimes figured as a major obstacle preventing an early meeting between contending parties. Special tables have had to be built before the process of mediation could even begin. At least in these cases the problem was recognized in advance. Provision of a wrong table might have the insidious effect, if the dangers are unrecognized, of prejudicing the outcome of meetings.

There are a few general rules that seem to be acknowledged about tables and the people who sit at them. Long rectangular tables are suited to hierarchically organized groups. If dining etiquette is anything to go by, status is measured by the inverse of the distance between the seated member and whoever is at the head of the table. Unstructured groups with little differentiation in status between members generally prefer a round table. A triangular table, on the basis of logic alone ought to commend itself to a management trio with members of roughly equal rank, were it not for aesthetic objections to such a disconcerting tripod. Otherwise the hierarchical trio suggests a boss behind a desk facing two subordinates, an arrangement that is possible in practically every office.

Less is known about the merits of other tables, such as ovals or rectangular tables with rounded ends.

What then can be said about the type of table suited to the management team of ideal size and composition? We had several ideas. One was that a bulbous table i.e. like a cross-section of a bulb with the top sliced off – not that we had ever seen one – might have much to be said for it. The table would be constructed in such a way that the chairman could have a commanding position where the bulb's growing tip, as it were, had been removed. The other members would have no overall positional advantage, for those nearer the chairman would have the advantage of physical proximity offset by not being able to see him as well as those further away.

At any rate we decided to try out the preferences of Henley members with six designs: a square, a circle, an oval, a rectangle, a rounded rectangle, and our proposed bulboid table. Members were invited to select the most favoured table and to pick their preferred position at the table assuming five other members were also to be seated. To our surprise we found that more people chose the round table than all the other tables combined and that this was true even when respondents were choosing the table at which they were to take the chair. The other notable result was the seating position chosen when the respondent was not in the chair. The majority favoured a position one seat removed fom the Chairman, a minority chose a seat opposite the chairman and only the odd claimant opted for a seat next to the Chairman. The rejection of a seat next to the Chairman shows how far removed are those rules that apply to seniority and status at dining table when the context changes to participating in executive decisions. Why this position should be so unpopular is open to speculation. Perhaps adjacency removes the potential intimacy of eye-to-eye contact. In many contexts, as in dining, a seat next to the Chairman offering the privilege of a word in his ear is considered an honoured location, much sought after by aspiring people. It seems to be another matter when decision-making is a social process and no longer depends on a single person.

If we need an operational definition of a management team we might propose that it is any group of executives favouring a round table for their meetings. A round table conveys the message that status and seniority should be discounted to enable each individual executive to contribute freely in accordance with his natural team-role. If the table is designed to sit between four and six people comfortably, the physical conditions are created to support a team "for all seasons". Now only one requirement remains – to find the right executives to occupy the vacant seats.

10:   Features of Teamsmen

Into the ark the managers went two by two. There were two types of negotiator (RI and TW), manager-worker (CW and CF), intellectual (ME and PL), and team leader (CH and SH). These ark members in all the various combinations of characteristics provide the basic material for populating the whole world of management teams. The RI is the creative negotiator; the TW, the internal facilitator; the CW, the effective organizer; the CF, the one who guarantees delivery; the ME, the analyser of problems; the PL, the source of original solutions; the CH, the team controller; and the SH, the slave-driver (where something stronger than control is needed). Management teams thrive on having members who are good examples of these types.

The diversity of personalities needed for a team raises the question therefore of whether those who are suitable have anything in common. Are there features that distinguish the effective teamsman, where teamsman can be defined as someone who readily finds a fitting part to play in the context of the team and always makes himself useful?

For many years during our experimental work we depended on observers to produce objective records of individual behaviour in teams. During the latter part of our studies we invited our observers to pick out individuals who in their opinion had made the most valuable contributions to the performance of the group. They were also asked to expand on how this had been achieved. There would have been a scientific advantage in asking them also to pick out the person who had contributed least or who had detracted most from the achievement of the group so that comparison might be made, but this we thought politically inadvisable. Some observers did spontaneously comment on members who in their view had been passengers in the team. In the main we built up a knowledge of effective teamsmen in terms of their positive qualities in an absolute sense rather than by comparison with poor teamsmen. In any case, we had plenty of examples of the latter from our own case study experience.

CONTRIBUTION AND TEAM-ROLE

Those identified as contributing most to team performance were drawn from the ranks of all the key team-roles. Marginally at the head of the list were those with Plant and Company Worker characteristics. Next on the list were Chairman-type members but only if these did at some stage secure the role of Chairman. Here several triumphs were scored by those who were not originally elected to take the chair but who came to the fore when the *company* was floundering and the members voted for job changes which in effect produced a new leadership. If that *company* then performed well the person in charge was often given the major share of the credit. His job would be that of Chairman but his team-role type would be different, approximating most closely to that of, say, Team Worker. Such a Chairman would foster a good team spirit and produce the climate in which the group could flourish. The greater the signs of early interpersonal difficulties, the more such a member was appreciated. Generally for a person to receive strong mention as a contributor it was necessary for the group to get into some sort of difficulty from which it could be rescued by the member with the abilities and personal qualities commensurate with the task. A mention would not necessarily imply that a nominated member was in essence an outstanding teamsman: it could be no more than that he was well suited to a particular situation. What was more convincing was when mention was combined with a description of the teamsman's skills so that these stood out as impressive in their own right.

From the sample of cases built up in this way teamsmanship was seen to transcend team-role. A good teamsman could adjust to a situation which called for a team-role he did not possess and yet he could still maintain his personal effectiveness. On the other hand someone with one strong team-role characteristic could be an asset to a team when matters flowed naturally in his direction but a liability as soon as his particular strength was no longer demanded by the situation. The late Charles de Gaulle would be an example of the latter. An example of the former might be the late Chou En-Lai, Prime Minister during much of the Mao Tse-Tung era, who succeeded in keeping the ship of state afloat whether in the waters on which a hundred flowers were blooming or amid the turbulence of the Cultural Revolution. While teamsmen vary in their natural abilities and team-roles there are certain generalizations that can be offered about them.

TIMING

Outstanding teamsmen have an ability to time their interventions. They seem able to judge the moment that is ripe for their emergence in the particular team-role in which they are able to contribute effectively. The rider is that they know when to keep silent. The silent phase is not a passive one in which they are "switched off"; because it is only by the maintenance of attention and interest during the silent phase that they can judge the moment at which their own contribution is likely to be most appreciated. Typically neither the compulsive talker nor the shy introvert possess this type of capacity for timing. For the compulsive talker every moment is the one ripe for personal intervention; for the shy introvert the moment at which to intervene is governed by occasional surges in self-confidence rather than the objective needs of the situation.

The importance of timing for teamsmen was well illustrated in a negative way by a certain Reg Scorer, a man of very wide experience. His test scores revealed particularly high mental ability and creative disposition. He was also strong in dominance and low in anxiety. Scorer appreciated the value of teams and declared great interest in the whole field of group psychology, which he could easily back up with appropriate quotations from published research.

On first meeting, Scorer's talents immediately commended themselves. After that reactions to him varied. Some people would maintain an amicable relationship, while others cooled rapidly. Within a team however, it became evident that team members collectively learned to gang up against him. His knowledge, wide experience and ideas tempted him to overplay his hand at every opportunity. A display of resistance in the form of scepticism merely stimulated him to redouble his efforts in marshalling his arguments, finding supporting evidence for his ideas and rebutting objectors. There seemed almost no subject that was immune to his winning points. Eventually Scorer found himself being boycotted. Information was withheld from him. Arguments were manufactured to be used against him. This seemed to become even more important than the pursuit of the collective goal.

Even more remarkable than the conspiracy which Scorer seemed to provoke against him was his failure to perceive the gathering indifference, and then hostility, that his behaviour engendered. Undisguised boredom, even yawning, did nothing to diminish the flowing wisdom that poured from his lips. To his credit he responded to the eventually poor performance of his team with some magnanimity being only too ready to blame himself for various oversights and mistakes. In fact Scorer's strategies on how problems should be tackled were basically sound. His prime misfortune was that others worked so badly in any team of which he was a member.

Plants generally figure amongst the most successful as well as the least successful teamsmen. It could be that Plants need a good back-up role, such as that of Team Worker or Monitor Evaluator. This brings us to the second feature that characterizes the effective teamsman: the ability to switch flexibly between different team-roles.

FLEXIBILITY

One leading industrialist, on the Boards of an exceptionally large number of companies, declared that he played a slightly different role in each company. Whether that was so or not could not be confirmed. We could, however, build up a dossier of authenticated material on one industrialist who rose eventually to the apex of managerial responsibility in a nationalized industry, and who was well known for his distinctive style of management.

Mervyn Hawley joined a large process industry as a young man having reputedly walked into the town, where a large factory offered many opportunities for employment, carrying all that he possessed with him. Mervyn was soon recognized for his enterprise and initiative and gradually climbed the ladder of responsibility until his own lack of qualifications became the main barrier to further advancement. At this point he decided to study for a degree in an appropriate technical subject while continuing his job. After his graduation he advanced rapidly within the organization, bypassing in promotion older graduates holding better degrees gained in the most prestigious universities, until he eventually found himself in command of tens of thousands of people.

Mervyn showed unusual skill in getting the most out of any team of which he was a member. Here his typical pattern involved three phases of operation. The first phase was the preparation of the ground. During this phase he had a habit of wandering about tracking down information to its sources. Wearing a white overall he would mingle with the shift workers, usually being taken for a laboratory assistant. Men asked for their views on issues connected with their work or questioned on points of work detail are only too happy to supply the answers if they are approached in the right way. Mervyn would arrive at meetings better prepared than his colleagues. At these meetings he was reluctant to declare what he already knew but instead favoured an informal discussion which gradually turned into a free-for-all. This second phase was a feet up on the table affair with any differences in rank or status totally ignored. Just when the possibilities and options seemed endless the second phase would end. Feet would come off the table, rank and authority reasserted themselves. Mervyn would make a decision and from then on it would be Mr. Hawley, the driving force, who would turn decision into unrelenting action.

Hawley's ability to interchange the team-roles of Team Worker, Resource Investigator and Shaper gave him a repertoire that fitted him well for a wide range of managerial situations. Nevertheless a change in team-role is not easy to bring about convincingly. Those who are capable of sudden switches need to signify to their colleagues which team-role they are now adopting. Dress and body language both have a part to play in this: some managers take off their jackets in discussion with colleagues when they need to dispense with the pressures and constraints that attach to rank and authority; equally they invoke them by returning to formality in dress when the occasion demands. Experienced managers find various means of signifying their team-role intentions. Spectacles can be put away to allow for more intimate eye-to-eye contact and to encourage communication; the lenses can be wiped to signify contemplation of the issues in question; or spectacles can be worn, even if there is no need for their normal usage in reading as a means of focusing the attention of the group on the gravity of the decision-making moment. In one large manufacturing establishment the Chief Executive wore a pair of pince-nez spectacles which he used in a flexible way to good effect for establishing the appropriate cues in role relationships. His ocular accoutrements were copied by other managers but although pince-nez became an emblem of management other managers failed to use them to the same good purpose!

SELF-RESTRAINT

If managers have more than one part to play in teams they will need to establish clearly the team-roles they intend to adopt, but they will also need to decide which team-roles they are *not* going to play. By limiting their own team-role ranges, they provide the opportunity for others to develop their own distinctive capabilities and in so doing the group is strengthened by the sense of community and common purpose that is produced by interdependence of effort. Some managers are as remarkable for what they refrain from doing as for what they do. The importance of this restraint is easily underestimated.

Peter Pointer was Chairman of a large industrial group having attained the position at an unusually early age. But Pointer was not a bright young whizz kid. Had others tried to model themselves on his apparent behaviour it would have been difficult to do so since there was not a great deal of overt management style that was available for imitation. The meetings over which he presided were well conducted. In the chair he made fewer interventions than the average intervention rate of others attending the same meeting. What distinguished Pointer's own contribution was his capacity to sum up. The summing up was not always a balanced account of what had gone beforehand but it did represent a judicious conclusion and verdict on the proceedings which no one ever challenged. In spite of Pointer's low contribution rate, as judged by volume, the meetings over which he presided had a reputation for solid achievement.

Self-imposed restraint is one way of opening up the field for others and so giving scope for the group to explore its latent resources. A more deliberate and sophisticated way of doing this is to create a team-role void which another is then invited to fill. The skilful teamsman will build up a specification of what is needed within the team if some important task is to be accomplished but declare a personal lack of qualification or skill for the task. The stronger the self-declaration of an inability to enter the role, the more powerful becomes the invitation to others to rise to the occasion. By acting in this way the teamsman stands in contrast to the typical careerist who is usually anxious to display his full range of skills at every opportunity. Yet the teamsman often overtakes the careerist in the promotion stakes because he builds up such strong support amongst colleagues.

A striking example of this type of teamsman approach was once told to me by an industrial executive recounting his experience in the navy. He had the good fortune as a young man in the services to work closely with an admiral. It soon became apparent to him that the admiral's management style contrasted with the pattern of styles that he had encountered amongst other officers in the navy. The initial impression was that the admiral was poorly endowed with grey matter. Instead of acting as the wise arbiter and decision-maker on all matters referred to him, which is what might be expected of an admiral, difficult problems were always referred to the clever young men on his staff. These young men busied themselves in furnishing the admiral with reports, graphs, and tables of figures in support of any opinion that they chose to offer when consulted. The admiral commonly reacted to the merest overload of information or hint of ambiguity with bewilderment. He would declare that he could not understand what a report meant. If it was possible to misinterpret a table of figures he would do so. Occasionally graphs would be held upside down. The bright young men learned to respond by writing more concise reports, marshalling their arguments better, and separating relevant from irrelevant data. The decisions taken, like all other matters connected with the admiral, had a habit of turning out well. In due course my informant had concluded that the admiral was not the stupid old buffoon he had originally mistaken him for, that he had a sharply critical mind, and that above all he had developed a fine technique for handling and developing a team of bright young men.

MAINTAINING TEAM GOALS

The skilled teamsman sets up others in appropriate team-roles for which he prepares the ground by creating a void into which they can enter. Clearly this approach can appeal to managers for different reasons. Letting others do the work does offer respite from personal effort and responsibility. The difference between exploiting other team members and developing them may not always be easy to discern; but it is important. Team success depends to a great extent on having members who set team goals above those of personal self-interest. The manager who is team-motivated will set up a role for others because it serves the wider purpose of the team and not for any ulterior motive. There are occasions when a job that needs to be done in a team is shirked by everyone within it. In that case the manager who places the interests of the team above his personal inclination to engage or not engage in a particular piece of behaviour will himself step into the breach. In other words the characteristics of the teamsman lie not so much in the jobs that he does or does not do but in the flexible ways in which he adapts his behaviour to cope with the needs of situations. Here he must learn to judge the capabilities of each member of the team in relation to the jobs to be done, treating himself on the same basis as others.

Some teamsmen distinguish themselves by their readiness to engage in undertakings that others avoid. They intervene merely because a job needs doing.

One manager with a great capacity for taking on unpopular jobs was Fred Blunt, the works manager of a large steel complex. Fred was a Yorkshireman who had risen from the ranks, furthering his education at night school during his rise through the middle echelons of management. Now, in the upper councils of the corporation, Fred contrasted with his colleagues in personality, outlook, and abilities. His colleagues had mostly enjoyed successful university careers followed by the company's investment in their career development; they had been moved from one post to the next and from one regional location to another in a logically conceived widening of their experience and responsibilities. Fred, on the other hand, was the local boy made good. No one had planned that he should reach his present appointment. It had just happened, though no one regretted it. Fred was certainly no intellectual but he had an inimitable way of coping with people and situations. He was regarded as an asset in a management team even by colleagues who crossed swords with him at regular intervals.

On one occasion the company was beset with an industrial relations problem which had persisted for an unacceptably long period. The managers concerned met to discuss how the problem might be resolved. In due course it became apparent that Spinks, the industrial relations officer most directly concerned with the affair, had not handled matters too cleverly. This was surprising since Spinks was a youngish university graduate quite able in his way, though evidently moved by sentiment and idealism rather than judgement. Once Spinks's mistakes had been catalogued it became evident that he was the weak link in the chain. He would have to be moved but there was no obvious position into which to move him. A temporary post might be found but the best solution was to get him to leave the company, which should cause him no great problem as he was, on paper, very marketable. With the exception of Fred, the managers at this meeting demurred at this solution. It would be too sudden. It might be seen as unfair. On the other hand it would be the ideal way out. "Has anybody told Spinks he has done a bad job?", asked Fred. The answers were vague and indefinite. No one had exactly told him. There had been several hints. It was very difficult. He always appeared pleasant and responsive when suggestions were made to him but nothing really changed. "Does he know that he has not done a good job?" said Fred. Further equivocations followed. "Right," said Fred, "call Spinks to my office. I'll see him now." That same day Spinks called at the Works Manager's office and by mutual arrangement his career with the company was terminated.

Fred Blunt was an amenable, popular manager, but unflinching whenever a difficult human situation had to be faced. Character counts whenever an important job lacks takers. In one case what is needed is moral courage; in another, exacting self-discipline; or in yet another, a readiness to endure tedium. A willingness to make a personal but well-judged sacrifice in the corporate interest is the mark of a teamsman. The mere wish to belong to social groups is often mistaken for and has little in common with this quality.

SUMMARY

In conclusion, teamsmanship can be viewed as something that transcends fitness for any particular team-role. Those who are nominated by others as "good to have in a team" have an ability to time their interventions, to vary their role, to limit their contributions, to create roles for others, and to do some of the jobs that others deliberately avoid. Whether these tendencies amount to skills or whether they are qualities of character is a moot point. The simple fact is that the natural teamsman is very likely to be enrolled into a team, even with the minimum of credentials, because he is seen as someone who pulls his weight and does nothing to detract from the contribution of others. Those who are organizing and composing teams may usefully pay as much attention to a candidate's teamsmanship as to any specialized ability he may possess.

11: Designing A Team

Management teams are commonly made up of members holding particular appointments. They are there by virtue of the offices or responsibilities they represent. No overall sense of design governs the composition of the group which, in human terms, is little more than a random collection of senior managers with as wide a spread of human foibles and personality characteristics as one might expect to find in the population at large. Nevertheless what we have established, or endeavoured to establish in this book, is that the compatibility of members of the management team is crucial to its effectiveness. It is a subject of no less importance than whether members of a team are talented as accountants, production engineers, or salesmen. The problem is that human compatibility is more difficult to assess than technical competence. Our experiments and fieldwork have given leads on how the subject of compatibility within the management might be approached. Methods and techniques will vary but some fundamentals remain unchanged. To guide us in our work of team design five interlocking principles can be set out:

1. Members of a management team can contribute in two ways to the achievement of team objectives. They can perform well in a functional role in drawing on their professional and technical knowledge as the situation demands. They also have a potentially valuable team-role to perform. A team-role describes a pattern of behaviour characteristic of the way in which one team member interacts with others in facilitating the progress of the team.

2. Each team needs an optimum balance in both functional roles and team-roles. The ideal blend will depend on the goals and tasks the team faces.

3. The effectiveness of a team will be promoted by the extent to which members correctly recognize and adjust themselves to the relative strengths within the team both in expertise and ability to engage in specific team-roles.

132

4. Personal qualities fit members for some team-roles while limiting the likelihood that they will succeed in others.
5. A team can deploy its technical resources to best advantage only when it has the requisite range of team-roles to ensure efficient teamwork.

OBTAINING INFORMATION

Acquiring reliable data about people is the starting point for effective team-building. Some thought therefore needs to be given as to how this may be done. The approach on which we mainly relied was the battery of psychometric tests, including some we had developed ourselves with the specific purpose of gaining the data we needed on team-role disposition and abilities. Some large companies well equipped with resources use comparable methods. The favoured approach is to collect the required information about people at the time of recruitment. This not only enables a firm to make a more informed decision as to whether a particular candidate should be taken on but also provides a data bank with good storage life offering a number of prospective uses: for example, the information can be used as an aid to career development. Individuals can be moved into positions where they are likely to fulfil themselves because their team-role capabilities fit the situation.

Another way of obtaining data on the team-role capabilities of intending team members is to use in-company training courses. Course participants learn about assessment methods and about those principles that govern the effectiveness of management teams. As they will wish to experience what is involved they are invited to complete two questionnaires on team-role, one based on self-perception (a form of this is given on pp. 153–7) and the other relating to the perceived team-role capabilities of known fellow participants. The information can then be used to form experimental teams on the training course. If the experience is rewarding participants may agree that the information has a constructive value and can be used in a wider setting to compose or recompose management groups or project teams. Clearly this can only happen where mutual trust prevails and when individuals are satisfied that any discrepancies regarding their personal team-roles have been satisfactorily sorted out.

Sophisticated methods and procedures are not, however, indispensable for forming well-integrated teams. Many firms evaluate their executives in annual assessments for the purpose of management planning and development. In other cases managers feel they know enough already about the people who report to them. What is lacking is not a sufficiency of information on the strengths, weaknesses and managing styles of those at the nucleus of the enterprise, but rather a tactical line on how to make better use of the information already available. Managers conversant with team-role theory have mentioned two ways in which they have changed their approach on simple, everyday issues.

RECRUITMENT

The first reported benefit relates to recruitment. When a new manager is being sought, what sort of person should the company look for? The orthodox, almost reflex response, is for a company to search for someone who fits the image of those who are already there. Fewer problems then arise in mutual adjustment between the newcomer and his established colleagues. But as we have already seen, the fact that assimilation is free of complications does not mean that the person being assimilated corresponds with what the organization needs. In team-role terms the more fundamental need is for someone who will fill the team-role gap in management. This cannot be ascertained without completing a team-role inventory of colleagues and examining what is missing. Once this is done a specification can be drawn up of the general shape of the candidate the firm would like to recruit. The interview now becomes directed towards the key question that the selectors will be posing to themselves: how far does the candidate match the personal specification?

INTERNAL RESHUFFLING

The second immediate benefit of using team-role concepts relates to internal postings. Managers have reported advantages in being able to make bolder moves than they would otherwise contemplate through confidence that the appointee will contribute the team-role that is lacking. This occurs typically where the experience which the incoming manager brings with him is not altogether appropriate but his natural orientation and behaviour more than compensates for any presumed deficiency in technical knowledge. The converse point is also reported as being important: internal postings that suggested themselves for technical reasons have been cancelled once the unpromising implications of the move in team-role terms have been explored.

   In these negative instances success cannot be claimed because no one can prove that mistakes have been avoided. It is easier to see errors of judgement in retrospect by re-examining cases where considerations of experience and technical competence have dominated the question of transfer to the exclusion of interpersonal considerations.

THE DANGER OF DESTROYING PARTNERSHIPS

A common mistake is to underestimate the dynamic factors that bind together the smallest team of all. Pairings of proven effectiveness are often broken up to fill managerial gaps or even as well-intentioned acts of management development, with little realization of how much the interdependence of two people contributes to the running of a successful unit. At one stage in my industrial career I witnessed an episode that had much to teach on the importance of these one-to-one relationships.

O'Hara first came to notice as the man running the office of a large production department in a company engaged in the extrusion and fabrication of plastics. One day the post of the manager of the department became vacant unexpectedly, the culmination, it must be said, of a number of production crises and turmoils that the department had been through. During this time one man had come to the fore as the only person who had made much progress in remedying the machine faults and effectively stemming the rise of scrap due to recurring problems. Sims was one of the fitters in the toolroom. True, he had been spotted before. In the preceding year the toolroom manager had been away ill and Sims had been put temporarily in charge. The experiment had not been a success, for Sims had merely carried on with his usual work and only involved himself with others in the toolroom when pushed into doing so. It was a great relief when the toolroom manager had returned. Nevertheless someone had to be put in charge of the department and with no other candidates in view a choice had to be made between O'Hara and Sims. The dilemma was whether to pick someone who was technically underqualified but skilful with people or to go for the technically most able man who had shown not the slightest inkling of management ability.

After much thought the job was offered, though not without some misgiving, to O'Hara. O'Hara accepted but did so on the condition that Silent Sims, as he was known to some, should be transferred to the department as the technical foreman. This was granted. The department now settled down to those familiar problems with which it had been long beset before the vacancy had arisen. However, within a few months all those indices that management uses to monitor efficiency began to register progress. This was remarkable since O'Hara and Sims had been part of the environment during those previous years when seemingly endless difficulties had been experienced.

The two men now struck up a close association and friendship within the department, while outside the department O'Hara was active in developing those contacts that extended his scope in the job. As time went on O'Hara forged links with the top rank of the company, frequently attending executive meetings. There, his natural fluency, unusual for works personnel, general charm, and sense of intimate knowledge about what was happening on the shop floor made a considerable impression. Only when it came to discussing options on unprepared gound did O'Hara become hesitant. He always wanted time to consult colleagues when conversation moved on to technical matters or complex policy issues.

Expansion of the business at last opened up the possibility of setting up a new automatic product line at Asheville, a factory some fifteen miles away. O'Hara was nominated factory manager. It seemed a natural choice. O'Hara was jubilant but put in a plea that Sims should come with him as technical manager. Unfortunately for O'Hara, Sims was considered indispensable where he was: he could have anybody else but Sims. This news seemed to depress O'Hara, but once over it and having adjusted to the inevitable he set about organizing the new factory with his characteristic vigour.

Eighteen months elapsed before I had occasion to visit the company again and could inquire how our two friends were faring. Sadly, their fortunes had risen only to fall. O'Hara had been quite unsuccessful as a factory manager, failing to get on top of any of the real problems. He was brought back to base as the Assistant Production Manager only to lose his job as part of a general cutback. Sims was still there, trouble-shooting on a new line, but no longer operating as a supervisor. The once flourishing partnership was dead, buried, and long forgotten.

Successful twosomes are more stable in top management than on the way up. A Chairman and a Managing Director who establish a good working relationship maintain it to the benefit of the enterprise as a whole. In contrast, any junior executive pair which does well will seldom be seen as anything other than two able individuals. Higher authorities will decide their respective destinies as they find themselves shunted into groups that are sometimes viable, sometimes not. Since role relationships are not readily discernible, they are likely to be ignored whenever career progression is being considered.

Sims and O'Hara, while their partnership lasted, could have formed the nucleus of a good team. But once their separation has taken place, who poses the more challenging problem in placement? Most personnel men would be drawn to O'Hara as the senior man. But where the purpose is to bring about effective team-building, Sims might make the greater claim for closer personnel attention. The argument is as follows: if managers possess general skills in being able to manage people, functions and businesses, it follows that they are more interchangeable than the specialists who report to them: good managers can be freely moved around and do not pose a major placement problem. That being so, it can become a better strategy to make a priority of finding a first-rate technical man for a department where technical factors are critical and then to find the manager who is most likely to fit in with him.

SEQUENCE OF SELECTION

This reversal of normal practice is the way in which we built up our most successful winning teams in the EME. We would start with an especially clever and creative individual or Superplant. Having selected him we then moved on to pick someone who would make a good team leader. The analogy in the world beyond management games is to look in the first place for a man of super talent in his field rather than for a manager.

Suppose a major new public building is to be erected which is to be not only functional but at the same time a monument of its kind. The first step is to search for an outstanding architect. Or take the case of a company which needs to build a special purpose machine to a demanding specification for its own internal use, but which could recover its development cost by serving a wider market outside the firm. Then it becomes necessary to find a design engineer of distinction before any further steps are contemplated. After that we may consider, in both cases, our next move – how the project shall be managed.

An alternative to the steps advocated would be to commission a consulting company dealing with architecture or with engineering design. This must be seen as second best. A company may only be as good as its stars. The experience may be not dissimilar to going back to a hotel renowned for its cuisine, only to find that its talented chef had left six months earlier. No company that supplies a service can be taken on faith until one knows more about the talents of the key person who, in the last analysis, will be most intimately connected with meeting the needs of the client.

If we revert to the project within the firm, the proposal to pick the best specialist or the most suitable genius to begin with, and to follow this with choice of a project leader, is open to the objection that, providing the sequence is not made public, one ends up with the same people anyway. The selection of A to be accompanied by B gives us the same pairing as starting with B and attaching to him A. To some the sequence in decision-making is seen as being immaterial to the decisions ultimately made. This we find to be as untrue as the notion that if two moves are to be made in chess it matters little which is played first.

Handling Specialists

Composing a team is a delicate balancing operation. If A is the designer, the specialist, the brains behind the business, the man on whose genius the success of the project depends, then everything else is conditioned by the first appointment. It is possible that this key person may possess managerial talent himself. It is more likely that he will not. He may be very deficient in managerial ability, while being insistent that he has it and unwilling to relinquish power. On the other hand, he may be only too glad to have another to take over the stressful managerial role in his job, leaving him free to concentrate on creative professional work. The key figure around whom the team is to be built will need to be managed in a particular way. To lay the foundations of a relationship which will allow creative potential to flourish may demand coaxing or controlling, humouring or restraining, assisting or driving. Our key figure may be exceptionally anxious and timid or he may be aggressively territorial, ever suspecting that he is about to be robbed of his invention or ideas. He may be brilliant but lazy or he may be overactive and overbold, recklessly prone to gaffes and to antagonizing potential supporters. All that has a bearing on the choice of the person destined to manage him.

There are occasions when the key man in a technical sense is neither creative nor particularly clever; it is just that he possesses unsurpassed technical knowledge and experience. He is indispensable to a project team although he has none of the qualities of team members. These individuals we have referred to as specialists for which we use "SP" to denote the team type – we can scarcely talk of SPs as having a recognized team-role. SPs have characteristic psychometric test scores, being highly introverted and anxious. The first requirement of a manager, or in the case of a team a CH, is whether he can relate to and manage the SP. If the SP were a man of exceptionally difficult disposition or outlook, a suitable team leader might be someone in the CH/TW mould. There is then a danger that the sort of manager who can humour a SP and underpin his failure to communicate effectively with his fellows will end up by making too many concessions to him. The SP's experience may be overvalued and begin to distort the strategies that are pursued. The safeguard is to introduce as the third member into the team someone in the PL/ME mould who could challenge the SP where necessary on fundamental issues and put forward alternative proposals. The price that might have to be paid is a rise in the temperature of disagreements. Creative conflict can be very rewarding but only a thin line of demarcation separates conflict which can have positive effects from that which becomes seriously disruptive. Therefore to create a final balance one could recommend for such a team a fourth member who could hold the team together. Here a TW/CW might be an excellent choice. The team would now have the following design:

Specialist	Chairman/Team Worker
Team Worker/Company Worker	Plant/Monitor-Evaluator

We might make the general prediction that this team would be well equipped to tackle a technically very difficult project in a practical way and that while disagreements would be likely to break out, the team has the resources to settle its differences and to reach its goal.

Where teams can be drawn up without necessarily having to include a particular person the sequence in which members need to be considered for enrolment in a team becomes less important. Nevertheless sequence can seldom be disregarded.

DESIGN AND PURPOSE

Let us consider two types of team built for different purposes, each to contain five members. One team is needed to design a new model and prepare a prototype. Another is needed to streamline the system destined to produce it. In the case of the former a designer of genius may be required. Such a man would require someone of equal intellectual acumen whom he can respect, to monitor him and keep him under control. A good candidate for the job is found but neither he nor the designer look like managers. We now have to find a manager to "chair" the project, who will adopt a low profile and give those with the ability their heads. The favoured nominee has the personal controlling power to take on someone else under his wing. So one further person with creative talents, complementary to those of the first nominee, and a wide range of contacts seems worth enlisting. This last member is an acceptable person who is likely to work well with others but happens to be weak in follow up. This conditions the choice of the final member as a person with solid organizing ability who is also a meticulous finisher. The resulting well-balanced team, depicted with our team-role notation, is shown as Team I and can be compared in its composition with Team II. Here the emphasis switches away from the management of innovation towards getting things done at high speed in a politically sensitive area.

A DESIGN FORMAT FOR TWO FIVE-MAN TEAMS

Team I

Chairman/Team Worker

| Superplant | Monitor-Evaluator/Company Worker |
| Resource Investigator/Team Worker | Company Worker/Completer-Finisher |

Team II

Shaper/Completer-Finisher

| Monitor Evaluator/Team Worker | Team Worker/Company Worker |
| Company Worker/Team Worker | Completer-Finisher/Team Worker |

For Team I, richly endowed with talent and resources, the problem of management is primarily one of controlling the balance with no more than the occasional, though firm, touch on the tiller. Team II, on the other hand, calls for leadership from the front. Someone with relentless drive, who can be guaranteed to get results and ensure that schedules are met, is appointed. The group that is set up for this streamlining/ organizing project is essentially a support team around a leader. Each member is likely to possess skills that will compensate for and cover the team leader's bulldozing ability, while having something positive, probably of a technical nature, to contribute in his own right. Members of Team II are rather more similar to one another than members of Team I but in the circumstances that is inevitable. Had our leader been depicted as belonging to the SH/TW type, an unlikely but not impossible combination, there would here seem less merit in constructing a support team. Other team-roles might have been introduced which would have had the effect of offering more competition with the leader from within the team.

INDIVIDUAL ROLES AND TEAM-ROLES

The question of the interaction of members within a team becomes more important the more often a team meets. But what happens when a team meets only rarely? Everyone is busy doing his own particular job and it is the interplay of work that constitutes the team effort rather than the effectiveness in combination when the members convene as a group. Now the likelihood of role clashes diminishes but the question of team-role coverage remains just as important. Members of a team will be assigned separate tasks consistent with their team-role characteristics and they will meet formally only when the tasks are done or near completion.

> Consider the case of a firm which is about to embark on a major programme of re-equipment. Decisions about which machines to buy will have a crucial effect on the future of the company. The available equipment varies in sophistication, reliability, capacity, price and even in terms of what is known for sure about its specification and performance. Some of the overseas machines seem very advanced and call for a visit. This is especially so in the case of one firm with a technical brochure that nobody can understand even after translation. How do we approach the subject?
>
> The first problem is to find someone who has a detailed knowledge of the merits and demerits of the equipment under consideration. Eventually an expert is traced belonging to the advisory service of the Trade Research Association. He seems very well-informed but less impressive in other ways.

Our starting nucleus then is our SP. We ask him to report to the Chief Engineer who is a ME. Together they draw up a shortlist of the firms and machines worth visiting. Our best RI is the Marketing Manager who is going to the States next month anyway. He can be talked into getting hold of the details that SP and ME require by visiting the machine manufacturers during the course of his trip. If all goes well he can do the same with those European counterparts still on the shortlist. A meeting is now convened by the Manager who is a CH. In addition to the SP, ME and RI he invites in a PL (the Research Manager) and a CF (the Quality Controller). The pros and cons of the various machines are thrashed out and eventually a decision is made to send the SP to two of the specified manufacturers to take a more detailed look at the machines. If his reports are favourable he will be followed by the CF who will check on their performance under operating conditions. A final plan is drawn up whereby one best buy will be ordered and assessed for a period of two months by the ME. After that a decision will be made at a formal meeting of the team on the big order.

It is evident that people may work as a team without being part of a working group. Conversely people may belong to the same working group without constituting a team. The essence of a team is that its members form a co-operative association through a division of labour that best reflects the contribution that each can make towards the common objective. The members do not need to be present at the same place and at the same time to enable the team to function.

Good teams would be much easier to form in industry for project work or management meetings if thought were given to the team-role composition of natural working groups. In practice there are a multitude of reasons why well-balanced teams are unlikely to form spontaneously. People are often picked for working groups because they are sensed as having characteristics akin to those who are already there, as discussed in Chapter Three. So redundancies in some team-roles will be associated with shortages in others. At higher levels of responsibility similar team-role types are found because the organization favours and rewards with promotion those with particular styles of approach.

TEAMS IN STATIC STRUCTURES

One of the prime obstacles is that a rigid hierarchical structure precludes entry into the team of the most suitable individuals. This raises the question of how a good team can be formed in an organization which is not recruiting nor likely to transfer people from the jobs they currently hold.

The suggested approach here is to avoid building teams on the basis of *ex officio* appointments. A meeting of heads of departments, for example, can all too easily turn into a gathering of Shapers with disastrous results. It is often better to set up a project or study team following the principles of team design drawing on people at different levels in the hierarchy. Such a team will not have the same authority as one drawn from functional heads of the organization but it is likely to be more effective. What is then needed, however, is a way of relating the project team to the organization so that its work may gain the backing of the organization as a whole, for the project will have little standing in its own right. Where the members of a project team are not nominees of departments but the appointees of whoever forms the team, there is a political as well as a consulting need to involve heads of departments. The most convenient way of doing this is to convene a project steering group that will meet occasionally and briefly advise the project team on guidelines and objectives. The reporting structure can allow each team to report to the Chief Executive. By this means the ideally constituted project team is assured of its independence; it cannot be killed by any members of the hierarchy who are wedded to existing practice.

CONCLUSION

Establishing the right climate in which well-designed teams can form and flourish is the foundation stone on which more effective teamwork in the future can be built. Only then does it become possible to explore the many questions raised by trying to create an optimum combination of people. The merits of each potential member can be raised in terms of what technically he can contribute and the role that he is likely to play in the group that is being formed. Once this process starts one finds that some people have more to contribute than others irrespective of what it is they have to offer. Designing a team engenders a search for individuals who are good examples of their type. A creative member needs to be very creative rather than moderately so; a tidy-minded, reliable individual may be appreciated for good finishing qualities but rather less so than someone of restrained disposition but a compulsive need to get things done.

Designing a team rests on a limited number of principles and concepts and involves various methods and techniques. But what turns team-building into an art is that the bricks, like legendary men, are made of different types of clay and not wholly predictable after firing.

12: Teams In Public Affairs

The last experiment in our joint programme of work with Henley in composing management teams was sober and subdued as happens when wonder ceases, the expected comes to pass, and the moment for departure arrives. We had learned much about the problems to which one should attend in putting a team together and thought the time was ripe to disseminate the message.

As we proceeded in this direction we came across a growing number of interested parties in the area of public administration. Here was a dilemma. Our experience had been largely founded on experimentally formed *companies* competing against each other to achieve a financial outcome the measure of which gave us a yardstick of effectiveness. On one hand, what we had learned seemed most appropriate to private enterprise and less applicable to undertakings that operate with non-commercial objectives. On the other hand, there was the view that the financial outcome was no more than a convenient means of measuring team effectiveness. The success or failure of these teams depended on certain principles. Could the lessons derived from them be put to good use in the management of public affairs? Such an approach might entail examining the key areas in the planning and decision-making process; ensuring that individuals with key skills got into teams of the right size where their abilities could be used to advantage; and training selectors in methods for forming teams with an adequate team role balance (amongst the other balances that would also need to be taken into account). If that task were undertaken rigorously, government might operate more efficiently whether at national or local level.

STRUCTURE AND POWER IN GOVERNMENT

Such an approach would be easy in principle if government had a clear-cut management structure and a simple reporting system. But it does not. In comparison with industry, public affairs in democratic society suffer not only from the drawback of being inherently more complicated but also from being conducted in a less orderly fashion. The onlooker is often uncertain as to where the vital decisions are made and this uncertainty usually is not far from the reality.

The late Aneurin Bevan, reflecting on his political career, saw his life as a journey in search of the place where real power lay; and declared at the end that he never found it. We too were reminded of the elusive nature and locus of power and responsibility during a visit to Canberra following an invitation to conduct a seminar on the running of management teams for the Public Service Board.

> Canberra is one of the few purpose-built capitals of the world, originally no more than a small rural town before being transformed into a landscaped city of 200,000 people on a scale that does justice to the size of the Australian continent. This great centre of government seemed the obvious place in which we might find answers to our long-stored questions on public policy and strategies for coping with problems that Australia shares in common with other developed countries. In spite of being personally taken round Canberra by a member of the Prime Minister's office and availing ourselves of introductions to many co-operative people, no answers were forthcoming to our principal questions and we were referred instead to the State capitals from which we had already come. This caused no surprise to our Australian colleagues. The image of government is of power emanating from a central core but the closer one gets to that core the more amorphous it becomes. The purpose of this capital city was more difficult to envisage and appreciate by visiting it than by viewing if from afar.

Some may consider it a good thing that power with its corrupting influence is not concentrated too strongly at any one point. Some loss in centralized authority, however, unless it is accompanied by the devolution of power, creates a kind of managerial vacuum. Matters that demand urgent attention lie beyond the scope of any given body or person, or even when they can be tackled they fall uncomfortably in the interstices between departments, where established machinery finds it difficult to function efficiently.

Bigness creates its own problems which are familiar to most large organizations. But the government suffers from both bigness and complexity in that it rests on an uneasily poised partnership between representatives elected to public office and those for whom public service is a career. The conventional picture is that politicians present a competing set of choices to the electorate from which those who are successful receive, collectively, a mandate to govern; it is then up to the civil servants to turn policies into practical programmes. Who then are better able to form the ideal policy-making team?

POLITICIANS AND TEAMS

Constitutionally, the reply must be the politicians if they are viewed as the senior members of the partnership and as acting in the role credited to them by the public. On this premise let us consider how in the conduct of public affairs we could ever hope to end up with our basic requirements for success: that is, a policy-forming and decision-making management team of ideal size with a well-balanced distribution in team-role capabilities amongst those who form the team.

Here we run into inevitable difficulties. Political practices are bounded by sets of well-established constraints. In the first place there is virtually nothing that can be done about unit size. The whole system is built upon a certain ratio between electors and elected. The constituency dimensions are fixed. The numbers who assemble in their council chambers are virtually constant. Each Parliament, Senate or Congress or its equivalent in any country of the world, will comprise several hundred representatives. In the United Kingdom there are over 600 Members of Parliament. This number is about one hundred times bigger than the ideal for formulating the most well conceived policies.

Conventions

Now the argument may be put forward that policies are authorized by Parliament but actually have their origins in party conventions. Here again familiar problems stand in the way of our requirements. The conventions themselves tend to be oversize and their agendas concentrate on traditional subjects that are treated in a general way. It is perhaps as well that this is so. The occasional attempt to formulate very specific programmes is usually resisted by those who must ultimately bear political responsibility. Large meetings are not the place at which judgements can be reached on difficult issues. Quite apart from the matter of size, the mood of such meetings is seldom one which favours dispassionate analysis and balanced decision-taking.

Committees

Many important decisions are taken, it is true, in committee where the "noise" problem associated with big meetings is partly overcome. Nevertheless, the committee is to some extent the microcosm of the whole. The problem of producing coherence in both argument and approach will be lessened but will still remain. The smaller group will make for more meaningful exchange of views but the prospects of a co-ordinated approach are hardly improved. Members of a political group or committee will retain their individualism; they are there to press a case or to give expression to a viewpoint with which they are associated in the wider world. This pursuit of a special interest is incompatible with what a team requires. A team differs from a group in that it demands from its members personal adjustment in playing one of a limited number of parts that together form an effective pattern. People need to be structured into a team. In how many political groups or committees is there a structuring force or a selector there to decide or to advise on what type of members are needed and what part they are to play?

Let us now put aside the question of how well policies are likely to be prepared before politicians enter office and consider instead the position that arises on their arrival. Here we may ask: what team-roles are they likely to fulfil?

Direct evidence is lacking but there are at least some leads. We have only to consider how politicians are selected in the first place to realize what qualities they will bring with them.

Likely Roles

What governs politicians' rise to the political forefront is the ability to create a sense of mission, to kindle enthusiasm about the things that people value; it is the ability to project hopes, to sense and respond to the mood of the public; it is the ability to use persuasive skills and energy in getting things done over a wide-ranging field. Here we have an evident specification for Shapers and Resource Investigators. Such people are likely to be highly extroverted and continuously on the go. They will be typically better at coping with emergencies and in responding to events in the short term rather than the long term. Sir Harold Wilson neatly encapsulated the temporal dimensions of the world in which politicians live: "a week is a long time in politics".

The inner qualities of politicians, the pressures to which they are subject and the circumstances in which they operate in day-to-day life are hardly conducive to membership of the small effective policy-making teams that we have in mind. Rather it is easier to see them fulfilling themselves as guardians of the political process and as managing the political scene.

CIVIL SERVANTS IN TEAMS

That being so, let us turn to examine their partners in government. The test results of Civil Servants who attended Henley over the years brought out two general points: firstly, they tended to be similar to corporate planners in industry but differed from other industrial managers by being more introverted; and secondly, a good proportion scored well on the measures of mental ability. This latter point is in line with the stringency of the examinations that they are required to pass in order to enter the Civil Service in the first place.

These criteria help to set the scene for the two "clever" team-roles, Plant and Monitor-Evaluator. Here again, as might be expected, these two team-roles – and especially the latter – were well represented. Neither of these team-role types would fit easily into the political scene. The creative ideas man is in danger of falling foul of the political consensus that binds a party together, whereas in the Civil Service he can be hidden away in a back room. The prospect of a political career looks no more promising for the classic Monitor-Evaluator. Dry, dispassionate and slow-moving souls are not the stuff of which political candidates are made. Company Worker and Team Worker team-roles also figured amongst the Civil Servants, as might be expected for those in administrative functions, but Shapers and Resource Investigators were under-represented.

When it comes to promotion the ability to play an effective part in a team, where the important decisions on departmental matters are made, is among the factors taken into consideration for the higher ranking jobs. Once in these jobs Civil Servants are able to control the size of teams in which they operate without external constraint. All in all Civil Servants have a starting advantage when it comes to forming effective policy-making groups.

The paradox, then, is that politicians and senior public servants are in many respects better fitted for the critical aspects of each other's ostensible duties. Senior public servants have the time, inclination, and natural ability to formulate new policies. Politicians, on the other hand, have the drive and energy and the persuasive skill to turn policies into acceptable forms of action.

EXCHANGE OF ROLES

It is true, of course, that a certain amount of exchanging of roles goes on once politicians enter office. The formal and informal systems diverge under pressures that are created. Those in political life attend so many functions that they are obliged to leave some policy considerations to officials, while still retaining the outward appearance of being in charge.

> Some insight into the nature of the relationship between Civil Servants and politicians has been afforded us over the years using Cambridge as a vantage point. This opportunity has come about partly because of our close link with two Ministries, but partly also because Cambridge is a major conference centre at which Government Ministers often make widely quoted policy statements at the conferences they address.
>
> A recurring observation is that it is rare for a Government Minister to write his speeches except where he is addressing his own political supporters. On one occasion a Minister was accompanied by three faceless officials, none of whom overtly seemed to play any part in the proceedings. This trio was taken aback by the unexpectedly bold question: "Which of you wrote the speech?" The answer came in one raised hand, a delighted smile, and the counter-question: "Did you like it?" The speech writer turned out to be the most junior member of the travelling hierarchy with the other two members being the writer's immediate superior and the Minister's personal assistant.

The strength of hand of those within public administration is indicated by the fact that some Ministers never meet the individuals who write their speeches. In these cases the shadow writer will occupy a more humble position than one who is close to the Minister: yet while he languishes in obscurity, he enjoys in effect remarkable power and influence. An account from a well-informed source of the origins of one of the most important pieces of post-war industrial legislation illustrates the route by which new policies can see the light of day.

> One day a young Oxford graduate was given the task of writing a speech for a Minister who was to address an industrial conference. This imaginative young man in his innocence drew on a number of ideas of his own that had not even been discussed with his superiors. He elaborated on these ideas in commendable but unsupervised prose while his boss was away on holiday. The text was typed and duly placed on the Minister's desk. When the shadow writer's superior realized how far the junior had overstepped the mark he attempted to get the speech withdrawn for revision. "No, I like it," the Minister told him. So the speech was given as it stood. The salient point was picked up by *The Times*. Journalists speculated. The Minister defended "his" position while treating the matter as being "under consideration". In due course there was a change of Ministers but the matter was now firmly established on the agenda of the Ministry and in due course a bill was introduced and became law.

Policies that originate with officials carry the advantage that they will certainly be vetted by Ministers and accepted, modified or rejected.

There are possibilities here of building up an effective working relationship, with the twin arms of government recognizing the part that each can best play. The story about the young Oxford graduate however does not illustrate typical practice but was told to me by an official precisely because it represents an aberration of the system. Government is not supposed to work like that.

IMBALANCE IN GOVERNMENT

A team-role approach to government could involve both its professional and political arms in an embracing operation around the generation of ideas, assessment, and decision-making. The last of these three processes is peculiar to elected representatives. Balance can be achieved only if the other two processes precede the third and have a fair degree of independence. Constitutional orthodoxy, based on total political control over government, is susceptible to producing a systems imbalance since there is no checking mechanism. This danger is especially liable to occur in the many instances when plans are conceived at the political level without the support of a professional management team to formulate the project and assess its feasibility.

At the time of writing this chapter the publication of Peter Hall's *Great Planning Disasters*, with case studies from the United States, Britain, and Australia, brings out the massive consequences of intrepid initiatives by politicians acting alone or in concert. An example is the Anglo-French Concorde, described by Hall as "perhaps the costliest commercial blunder in history", though for sheer rate of cost escalation it scarcely rivals the Sydney Opera House. Concorde began as a report on supersonic transport by a committee entirely composed of air interests. The report in itself scarcely constituted a project and was never even made public. Yet the Minister responsible acted boldly as he explained with disarming frankness to a House of Commons Expenditure Committee:

"It was quite clear to me that were I as Minister to go to the Treasury the money would not be forthcoming. So in June, 1959, I went to France and I took advantage of the then Paris Air Show to suggest to the French that they should co-operate with the British in developing Concorde. It was in this way that I started. In retrospect I have to admit that my Department and I had no knowledge at all and had made no attempt at all to estimate the size of the potential market."

The need to find a new aircraft to keep the ailing British aircraft industry busy, after a history of cancelled aircraft; the importance of the aircraft workers' vote when after a change of government a new Minister was appointed who was also the parliamentary representative of the

constituency where Concorde was being built; and the belief
(mistaken, as it happened) once the dire facts of the project began to
emerge, that continuation with Concorde was the price that Britain
had to pay to appease Charles de Gaulle's opposition to Britain's entry
to the European Common Market, were all factors that kept Concorde
alive.

Many projects and programmes that are entirely political in origin
have an unhappy ending. It is not uncommon for them to result in effects
which are the exact opposite of what was intended. Measures to protect
tenants or indigenous industries, for example, have all too often
increased their ultimate plight. It is not that political sincerity or the will
is lacking. Political reverses have much to do with the failure to forecast
how isolated measures will affect the system as a whole: any disturbance
may be nullified or even overcompensated for by the stimulus given to
counterbalancing forces. Electorally attractive but oversimple solutions
to problems may founder on the hard bedrock of reality. Yet the real
crisis in government has less to do with adversity in itself than with what
ensues from setbacks. It is in the nature of things that politicians never
have fallback programmes. To proclaim an open change of line would
be to risk the disaffection of supporters and to prepare a path into the
political wilderness. What therefore happens is that political dictation of
policy gives way to a sudden loss in political control and direction.
Power and responsibility begin to seep back, as inconspicuously as
possible, into the hands of permanent officials. These, being more *au fait*
with the affairs of state, less subject to day-to-day pressures, and
enjoying long-term rather than transient appointments are well placed
to come up with their own saving line. This is not the way government is
intended to operate. Nor has such a sequence much to commend it from
the point of view of efficiency.

The reasons why politicians are so difficult to weld together into
efficient teams have been discussed earlier. Yet there is one exception to
the rule that does not conflict with what has been learned about
successful teams during our studies. This exception centres on the
principle of a team supporting a single but elected figure.

PRESIDENTIAL GOVERNMENT

The merit of a presidential style of government is that whoever is
successful is able to create his own team. The ideal arrangement leaves
him free to go outside the ranks of his colleagues (and possible rivals)
and to select those with whom he can establish a close and effective
working relationship. The American system of Presidential primaries

offers a particularly interesting example of how two basically conflicting systems can be combined to this end. Candidates and their teams are presented to the electorate for their initial choice as a prelude to the binary choice that occurs later in the Presidential election. A single powerful figure with an effective back-up team can take full advantage of opportunities but equally can succumb to the most dangerous risks. Some of the teams formed on this pattern in our experiments were amongst the most successful but others of them were conspicuous amongst those producing the worst results.

The Presidential primary system offers an extra sifting of candidates that allows the electorate more choice in selecting an ultimately powerful figure and his team, improves the likelihood of a favourable outcome, and is therefore a brilliant assay at a difficult problem. If, however, we were to apply the principles of team design to the management of public affairs, the Presidential system and its local equivalents are not to be recommended with confidence. Instead, we would prefer the balanced team of the type that has triumphed so well in our experiments. In that team it is not the Chairman (or the President) who is the dominant figure. The Chairman is no more than a man-manager who draws on the resources of a talented group. The focus shifts across from the cult of a personality with his aides to the potential of the team as a whole.

TEAM-ROLE INTERACTION

Accordingly, our preferred suggestion for the better management of public affairs is for a change in role relationships within government. To this end, its political arm should primarily concern itself with final decision-making, with supervision of its Ministries, and with enhancing its special responsibilities for close contact and communication with the public. In so doing, it should disengage from the demanding task of developing detailed plans to meet major problems. This intricate and often slow operation is better handled by those who are able to control the group size of their own teams; who can heed individual performance assessed in previous tasks; who can take account of team-role balance, and who can ensure that members have the qualities that match the team-role for which they are envisaged: in other words, the permanent employees of government meet this specification better than the elected political representatives themselves. If this is so, there is much to be said for readjusting the relative responsibilities of elected representatives and government officials. Each group needs to be deployed in a way that is most fitted to the service it can render.

We might then reach this conclusion: democracy is likely to run into operating difficulties, where the intent is that the maximum numbers of people participate in the decision-making process and equally where that authority is transferred to overworked elected representatives who are expected to assume the total responsibilities of government. Government in practice depends on both elected representatives and career officials. It is only through building up a pattern of interlocking accountability, widely recognized and accepted, that democratic government can function efficiently.

Public servants are not expected to produce plans and options in their own right, for they are regarded as being primarily there to enact decisions that are already made. Yet the lessons of industry teach us that new developments seldom succeed unless those responsible for their execution also have an active part to play in planning what is to be done. It is far better that this role is overt rather than surreptitious. And if it is overt the political arm of government must change to allow it to focus more on the management of the mandarins. Politicans might then do better to concentrate on priorities and decisions; and mandarins, on policies and plans.

Better government is essentially about how different groups of people with different terms of reference can work within a common structure. And within that structure it is about how teams are best formed to make each group more effective. Any society that develops such an arrangement; that learns as part of that process how to construct the right teams of people, of whom to ask the right questions, and how to take advantage of the answers, is set fair to promote its own well-being.

A Self-Perception Inventory

This inventory was developed from a number of earlier versions which had been designed to give Henley members a simple means of assessing their best team-roles.

DIRECTIONS: For each section distribute a total of ten points among the sentences which you think best describe your behaviour. These points may be distributed among several sentences: in extreme cases they might be spread among all the sentences or ten points may be given to a single sentence. Enter the points in the Table on p. 156.

I. What I believe I can contribute to a team:
   (a) I think I can quickly see and take advantage of new opportunities.
   (b) I can work well with a very wide range of people.
   (c) Producing ideas is one of my natural assets.
   (d) My ability rests in being able to draw people out whenever I detect they have something of value to contribute to group objectives.
   (e) My capacity to follow through has much to do with my personal effectiveness.
   (f) I am ready to face temporary unpopularity if it leads to worthwhile results in the end.
   (g) I am quick to sense what is likely to work in a situation with which I am familiar.
   (h) I can offer a reasoned case for alternative courses of action without introducing bias or prejudice.

II. If I have a possible shortcoming in teamwork, it could be that:

153

(a) I am not at ease unless meetings are well structured and controlled and generally well conducted.
(b) I am inclined to be too generous towards others who have a valid viewpoint that has not been given a proper airing.
(c) I have a tendency to talk a lot once the group gets on to new ideas.
(d) My objective outlook makes it difficult for me to join in readily and enthusiastically with colleagues.
(e) I am sometimes seen as forceful and authoritarian if there is a need to get something done.
(f) I find it difficult to lead from the front, perhaps because I am overresponsive to group atmosphere.
(g) I am apt to get too caught up in ideas that occur to me and so lose track of what is happening.
(h) My colleagues tend to see me as worrying unnecessarily over detail and the possibility that things may go wrong.

III. When involved in a project with other people:
(a) I have an aptitude for influencing people without pressurizing them.
(b) My general vigilance prevents careless mistakes and omissions being made.
(c) I am ready to press for action to make sure that the meeting does not waste time or lose sight of the main objective.
(d) I can be counted on to contribute something original.
(e) I am always ready to back a good suggestion in the common interest.
(f) I am keen to look for the latest in new ideas and developments.
(g) I believe my capacity for cool judgement is appreciated by others.
(h) I can be relied upon to see that all essential work is organized.

IV. My characteristic approach to group work is that:
(a) I have a quiet interest in getting to know colleagues better.
(b) I am not reluctant to challenge the views of others or to hold a minority view myself.
(c) I can usually find a line of argument to refute unsound propositions.
(d) I think I have a talent for making things work once a plan has to be put into operation.
(e) I have a tendency to avoid the obvious and to come out with the unexpected.

(f) I bring a touch of perfectionism to any team job I undertake.

(g) I am ready to make use of contacts outside the group itself.

(h) While I am interested in all views I have no hesitation in making up my mind once a decision has to be made.

V. I gain satisfaction in a job because:

(a) I enjoy analysing situations and weighing up all the possible choices.

(b) I am interested in finding practical solutions to problems.

(c) I like to feel I am fostering good working relationships.

(d) I can have a strong influence on decisions.

(e) I can meet people who may have something new to offer.

(f) I can get people to agree on a necessary course of action.

(g) I feel in my element where I can give a task my full attention.

(h) I like to find a field that stretches my imagination.

VI. If I am suddenly given a difficult task with limited time and unfamiliar people:

(a) I would feel like retiring to a corner to devise a way out of the impasse before developing a line.

(b) I would be ready to work with the person who showed the most positive approach, however difficult he might be.

(c) I would find some way of reducing the size of the task by establishing what different individuals might best contribute.

(d) My natural sense of urgency would help to ensure that we did not fall behind schedule.

(e) I believe I would keep cool and maintain my capacity to think straight.

(f) I would retain a steadiness of purpose in spite of the pressures.

(g) I would be prepared to take a positive lead if I felt the group was making no progress.

(h) I would open up discussions with a view to stimulating new thoughts and getting something moving.

VII. With reference to the problems to which I am subject in working in groups:

(a) I am apt to show my impatience with those who are obstructing progress.

(b) Others may criticise me for being too analytical and insufficiently intuitive.

(c) My desire to ensure that work is properly done can hold up proceedings.

(d) I tend to get bored rather easily and rely on one or two stimulating members to spark me off.
(e) I find it difficult to get started unless the goals are clear.
(f) I am sometimes poor at explaining and clarifying complex points that occur to me.
(g) I am conscious of demanding from others the things I cannot do myself.
(h) I hesitate to get my points across when I run up against real opposition.

POINTS TABLE FOR SELF-PERCEPTION INVENTORY

SECTION	ITEM a	b	c	d	e	f	g	h
I								
II								
III								
IV								
V								
VI								
VII								

To interpret the self-perception inventory you should now look at the Analysis Sheet opposite.

INTERPRETATION OF TOTAL SCORES AND FURTHER NOTES

The highest score on team-role will indicate how best the respondent can make his or her mark in a management or project team. The next highest scores can denote back-up team roles towards which the individual should shift if for some reason there is less group need for a primary team-role.

The two lowest scores in team-role imply possible areas of weakness. But rather than attempting to reform in this area the manager may be better advised to seek a colleague with complementary strengths.

Descriptions of the team-roles are given in the Glossary and there is a further table on page 78. The titles of the team-roles owe something

SELF-PERCEPTION INVENTORY ANALYSIS SHEET

Transpose the scores taken from the points table on the facing page, entering them section by section in the table below. Then add up the points in each column to give a total team-role distribution score.

SECTION	CW	CH	SH	PL	RI	ME	TW	CF
I	g	d	f	c	a	h	b	e
II	a	b	e	g	c	d	f	h
III	h	a	c	d	f	g	e	b
IV	d	h	b	e	g	c	a	f
V	b	f	d	h	e	a	c	g
VI	f	c	g	a	h	e	b	d
VII	e	g	a	f	d	b	h	c
TOTAL								

both to historical factors and to the need to avoid the preconceptions associated with established alternatives. These could not be entirely overcome and can therefore be misread. For example the Chairman team-role refers to the characteristics of Chairmen found in winning *companies* in the EME. In fact some successful Chairmen of industrial or commercial groups do not themselves adopt a typical Chairman stance but make their mark as Shapers, where sharp or rigorous action is the order of the day; or as Plants, where the Chairman's role is basically strategic.

Company Worker or Team Worker team-roles have tended to be undervalued because of their titles. The former has been replaced in some firms by the title Implementer but there is much to be said for Company Maker with its flavour of someone who acts as the backbone of the Company. As an alternative to Team Worker the term Team Builder has also been used. In practice some typical Company Workers and Team Workers in the business and industrial world become Chairmen of their firms. In these cases some aspects of their Chairman behaviour are learned, although other aspects of their style are likely to reflect their primary team-role.

Experience with the Self-Perception Inventory indicates that the most preferred team-role for executives is Shaper and the least preferred is Completer. We can therefore conjure up the image of the typical manager as good at initiating things, being pushy, outgoing and reactive, but weak in follow through. But such a conclusion should be treated with some reservation because in every questionnaire there is a tendency for some responses to be more popular than others. It is useful therefore to see how individual respondents compare with executives in general.

The Table of Norms below is based on scores of a cross-section of managers from various functions and industries.

TABLE OF NORMS FOR SPI (sample size = 78)

	Low 0–33%	Average 33–66%	High 66–85%	Very High 85–100%	Average score
CW	0–6	7–11	12–16	17–23	10.0
CH	0–6	7–10	11–13	14–18	8.8
SH	0–8	9–13	14–17	18–36	11.6
PL	0–4	5–8	9–12	13–29	7.3
RI	0–6	7–9	10–11	12–21	7.8
ME	0–5	6–9	10–12	13–19	8.2
TW	0–8	9–12	13–16	17–25	10.9
CF	0–3	4–6	7–9	10–17	5.5

NOTES ON *COMPANY* SUCCESS RATES OPPOSITE (SEE ALSO CHAPTERS SEVEN AND EIGHT)

The rank order in financial results ranged from *Company* D with the best result to *Company* F with the worst.

Neither the mental ability of the *company* as a whole nor the dominance of the Plant in providing ideas were important determinants on their own. On the other hand the observed working relationship between Plant and Chairman proved important.

In Company Worker teams, where Plants often faced problems of personal acceptance, the Chairman's support could have a major bearing on performance. *Companies* with Superplants or with extrovert members tended to do well.

In the case of *Company* A however a dominant Plant aggravated the Apollo effect.

COMPANY SUCCESS RATES WITH PLANTS IN DIFFERENT TYPES OF *COMPANY* (SEE pp. 34–5)

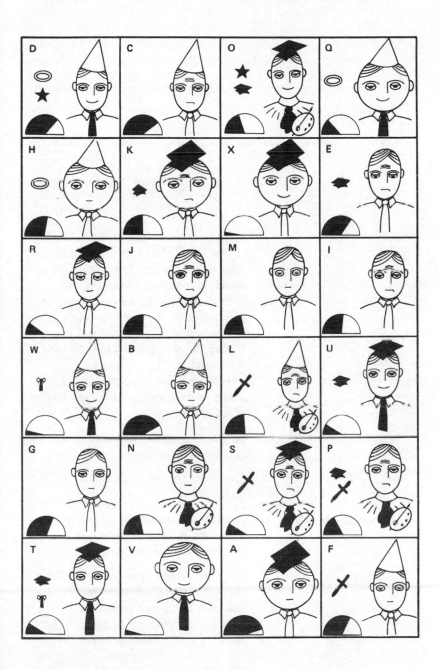

Glossary

Anxiety	Anxiety is measured on six scales of the 16PF. Anxious individuals are easily aroused. Where anxiety is allied with strong scores on self-control and discipline (measured on two scales of the 16PF) it tends to be converted into energy and drive. Where the discipline is low, anxiety is inclined either to exert an unsettling effect on others or to result in an unacceptably high level of inner stress.
Anxious Extrovert	Someone high in both anxiety and extroversion.
Anxious Introvert	Someone high in both anxiety and introversion.
Back-up Team-Role	A team-role to which an individual has some natural affinity other than his primary team-role.
Chairman	As a team-role, specifies controlling the way in which a team moves towards the group objectives by making the best use of team resources; recognizing where the

team's strengths and weaknesses lie; and ensuring that the best use is made of each team member's potential.

Company Worker

As a team-role, specifies turning concepts and plans into practical working procedures; and carrying out agreed plans systematically and efficiently.

Completer-Finisher

As a team-role, specifies ensuring that the team is protected as far as possible from mistakes of both commission and omission; actively searching for aspects of work which need a more than usual degree of attention; and maintaining a sense of urgency within the team.

Constructs

A set of related ideas and concepts which characterize an individual's outlook on the world. These are elicited by examining the pattern of discriminations an individual makes in sorting through material which is inherently capable of assuming different meanings. The development of construct theory owes much to G. A. Kelly and his *Psychology of Personal Constructs* (New York: Norton, 1955). Kelly's approach relied on a technique known as the Repertory Grid. This method, requiring a continuing intervention between a professionally trained person and a subject, tended to be too slow and costly for most industrial purposes. The PPQ was developed as an alternative method. The constructs of managers to which reference is made in this book refer solely to material generated by the PPQ. *Positive* constructs refer to reasons for liking something; *negative* constructs refer to reasons for dislike.

CTA (Critical Thinking Appraisal)

A test designed jointly by Goodwin Watson, Professor Emeritus of Social Psychology and Education of Columbia University, and Edward M. Glaser of Edward Glaser and Associates, Consulting Psychologists, Los Angeles. The CTA comprises five sections which measure Inference, the ability to discriminate beween degrees of truth or falsity from given data; Recognition of Assumptions, the ability to recognize unstated assumptions or presuppositions in given statements; Deduction, the ability to reason accurately from given statements or premises; Interpretation, the ability to weigh evidence and to distinguish between warranted and unwarranted generalizations; and Evaluation of Arguments, the ability to distinguish between arguments which are strong and relevant and those which are weak or irrelevant to a particular question at issue.

The CTA contains 100 items which have to be completed in 50 minutes, although in practice the time limit was not rigidly enforced. About 95% of respondents completed all items of the test. The offer was sometimes made of £10 to anyone who obtained full marks (or who got all items wrong!). This remained unclaimed as no one succeeded in achieving a perfect set of answers.

EME (Executive Management Exercise)

The EME was developed by Ben Aston at Henley as a management game. The aim was "to create a high-intensity reference experience that integrated many management skills that are otherwise treated on a fragmentary basis." The EME was an interacting game comprising between six and eight *companies*, each of which had six members. Performance depended not only on the decisions made within the *company* but on the decisions made by other *companies*, in respect of both the home and export markets. Financial returns, made available through a computer, gave results over a period of twelve "quarters" and the aim was to finish with the largest possible share of available assets. "Market Research" could be bought and decisions could be made on recruiting salesmen, advertising, investing in research, holding stocks and setting prices. The EME also made provison for transactions with "banks" and, in more recent years, for negotiations with "unions" and with "government". Over a decade the EME has undergone a period of continuous development but, whatever the differences, results have been generally a fair reflection of *company* or team effectiveness

Extroversion

Refers to a characteristic type of personality, first identified by Jung, whose interests are directed

outwards towards the external
world around them rather than
towards inner thoughts and
feelings. Measured by five of the
sixteen scales on the 16PF.

Extrovert

Someone high in extroversion.
Extroverts are now known to have
distinctive psychophysiological
characteristics tending to have high
sensory threshold levels. They
require more intense stimulation
for any given response and their
responses tend to fade relatively
quickly. Extroverts tend to become
bored easily or they adjust to this
susceptibility by keeping up a
continuous search for active
stimulation.

Functional Role

The role that a member of a team
performs in terms of the specifically
technical demands placed upon
him. Typically, team members are
chosen for functional roles on the
basis of their experience and
without regard to any personal
characteristics or aptitudes that fit
them for additional tasks within
the team.

Introversion

Discovered by Jung as applying to
a type of personality dominated by
inner thoughts and feelings rather
than by interest in the outer world
of men and things. Measured by
five of the sixteen scales of the
16PF.

Introvert

Someone high in introversion.
Introverts tend to have low
stimulus thresholds; they respond
strongly to small inputs of stimulus
and dislike strong stimulus

intensities. They do not get bored easily. Introverts tend to produce deep thinkers and highly creative individuals. They tend to be vulnerable to strong pressures.

Monitor-Evaluator   As a team-role, specifies analysing problems; and evaluating ideas and suggestions so that the team is better placed to take balanced decisions.

16PF   Otherwise known as the Cattell Personality Inventory. This test is a self-reporting questionnaire containing 187 statements in terms of which the respondent must choose between three possible answers. The 16 PF is so named because it comprises sixteen personality factors, albeit one of which covers intelligence. The remaining fifteen deal with dimensions of personality that are best known for the words that describe extreme scores at both ends of the dimensions, although these words can be misleading if scale is considered in isolation. The scales are reserved/outgoing, emotional/calm, humble/assertive, serious/happy-go-lucky, expedient/ conscientious, shy/bold, tender-minded/tough-minded, trusting/ suspicious, meticulous/imaginative, natural/shrewd, confident/ apprehensive, conservative/radical, dependent/self-sufficient, uncontrolled/controlled, relaxed/tense.

The 16PF generates a number of so called second order factors which combine scores from several scales. The second order factors referred to in this book are creative disposition, extroversion – introversion and anxiety – stability.

Plant

As a team-role, specifies advancing new ideas and strategies with special attention to major issues; and looking for possible breaks in approach to the problems with which the group is confronted.

PPQ

The initials of this test stand for Personal Preference Questionnaire. The test was developed by the Industrial Training Research Unit at Cambridge as a means of giving leads on personality and outlook that would be complementary to the information derived from a self-reporting questionnaire (i.e. the 16 PF). The PPQ is an open-ended test; in other words the respondent has to create his own responses rather than choose between given alternatives. The test comprises 50 pairs of well-known names (e.g. Mohammed Ali/Henry Cooper, Stan Laurel/Oliver Hardy), and the respondent is asked to indicate which of the pair is preferred and to give a reason (whether positive or negative) for making the choice. These reasons could be classified with the aid of a PPQ dictionary into five principal categories, each of which contains four sub-groups. The categories are Talent (sub-groups: Ability, Brain, Originality, Versatility); Achievement (sub-groups: Attainment, Competitive-ness, Determination, Consistency); Personality (sub-groups: Nice Guy,

Flamboyance, Social Capacity,
Humour); Justice (sub-group: Fair
Play, Integrity, Respectability,
Ethics); and Subjective Factors
(sub-groups: Clan, Physical
Reasons, Empathy, Reaction).
Scores in the sub-groups are
referred to as constructs.
Interpretation of the test scores is
facilitated by data available on
response norms in the sub-groups
for any total response level.

The PPQ is available in forms
that suit various countries and
different culture levels. So far there
are three UK, one international
(intellectual), one Australian, and
one Nigerian edition.

Primary Team-Role   That team-role to which an
individual has the greatest affinity.

Psychometric Tests   These refer to human facilities that
lend themselves to measurement.
Mental ability, personality,
character; and orientation can all
be examined by standard tests
which yield measured bits of
information. Although these tests
cannot cover every aspect of the
person, their advantage lies in the
standardized nature of the
information they yield. Individuals
can be compared with one another
on similar measures; the
information has good storage life,
is easily retrieved, and lends itself
to long-term research and
validation.

Resource   As a team-role, specifies exploring
Investigator   and reporting on ideas, developments and resources outside the

group; creating external contacts that may be useful to the team and conducting any subsequent negotiations.

Shaper

As a team-role, specifies shaping the way in which team effort is applied; directing attention generally to the setting of objectives and priorities; and seeking to impose some shape or pattern on group discussion and on the outcome of group activities.

Stability

Measured in six scales of the 16PF and in effect the opposite of anxiety. Stable individuals tend to be easy-going and acceptable to a wide range of people. They can also be casual and lazy and are unlikely to give of their best except under pressure.

Stable Extrovert

Someone high in both stability and extroversion.

Stable Introvert

Someone high in both stability and introversion.

Syndicate

A group of managers brought together to promote their mutual learning. Each syndicate at Henley contained ten or eleven members and lasted for the duration of the course.

Teamopoly

Teamopoly was developed as an experience offered to those attending management team seminars to enable them to put their newly acquired knowledge and insights into practice. Each *company* comprised four members, with either four or five *companies* taking part in the exercise which usually lasted five hours.

Teamopoly was founded on the principles of the well-known game Monopoly but there were some essential differences. All property could change hands only as a result of auction, tender, or negotiation. The moves were determined in advance and each *Company* was informed of its moves, so that it could assess their implications before each session of board play. A number of other changes to the rules minimized the element of luck in the game. The scheduling of activities created a great deal of pressure on the *companies* and this sense of pressure was made greater by composing *companies* in such a way that in human terms their membership was unbalanced and therefore likely to create difficulties. Since the game was of more limited character than the EME some members learned to live with these difficulties and to make personal adjustments (team-role sacrifices) in the interests of *company* performance.

Team-Role

This describes a pattern of behaviour characteristic of the way in which one team member interacts with another where his performance serves to facilitate the progress of the team as a whole. Only eight useful types of contribution were discovered. These were Chairman, Shaper, Plant, Company Worker, Team Worker, Monitor-Evaluator, Resource Investigator and Completer. Each of these team-roles was associated with characteristic types of personality as measured by the tests used in the experiments.

Team Worker

As a team-role, specifies supporting members in their strengths (e.g. building on suggestions); underpinning members in their shortcomings; improving communications between members and fostering team spirit generally.

Test Battery

A group of psychometric tests devised to measure in conjunction with one another some broad areas of human characteristics. The test battery used in these studies was put together to yield data that might usefully predict managerial performance and effectiveness. The constituents of the battery were the Watson-Glaser Critical Thinking Appraisal (Form YM), the Cattell 16PF (Form A, 1962 edition)—the 16PF 1967–1968 anglicized edition was abandoned as yielding less satisfactory data–and the PPQ.

Further Reading

Adizes, Ichak	*How to Solve the Mismanagement Crisis: Diagnosis and Treatment of Management Problems.* (San Diego: Adizes Institute, 1981)
Ardrey, R.	*The Social Contract.* (London: Fontana, 1971)
Bales, R. F.	*Interaction Process Analysis: a Method for the Study of Small Groups.* (Cambridge, Massachusetts: Addison Wesley, 1950)
Handy, C.	*Gods of Management.* (London: Pan Books, 1979)
Hollander, E. P.	*Leadership Dynamics.* (New York: The Free Press, 1978)
Janis, I. L.	*Victims of Group Think.* (Boston: Houghton Mifflin, 1972)
Jay, A.	*Management and Machiavelli.* (London: Hodder and Stoughton, 1969)
Jay, A.	*Corporation Man.* (London: Jonathan Cape, 1972)
Kellner, P. and Lord Crowther-Hunt	*The Civil Servants: an Inquiry into Britain's Ruling Class.* (London: Macdonald, 1980)
Likert, R.	*The Human Organization: Its Management and Value.* (New York: McGraw-Hill, 1967)
Lippitt, G. L.	*Organization Renewal.* (New York: Appleton-Century-Croft, 1969)
Margulies, N. and Wallace, J.	*Organization Choice.* (Glenview, Ill: Scott Foresman, 1973)

Mintzberg, H.   *The Nature of Managerial Work.* (San Francisco: Harper and Row, 1973)

Rackham, N., Honey, P.   *Developing Interactive Skills.* (Guilsborough: and Colbert, M. J.   Wellens Publishing, 1971)

Ramsden, P.   *Top-Team Planning.* (London: Cassell and Associated Business Programmes, 1973)

Woodcock, M.   *Team Development Manual.* (Farnborough: Gower Press, 1979)

Index